FAITH-DRIVEN LEADERSHIP

God's Blueprint for World-Class Business

JERRY HOWARD

Anchor & Light Press

Faith-Driven Leadership
God's Blueprint for World-Class Business

© Copyright 2025 by Jerry Howard. All rights reserved.

Published by Anchor & Light Press.

No part of this publication may be reproduced, distributed or transmitted in any form or by any means, including photocopying, recording, or other electronic or mechanical methods, without the prior written permission of the publisher, except in the case of brief quotations embodied in critical reviews and certain other noncommercial uses permitted by copyright law.

Although the author and publisher have made every effort to ensure that the information in this book was correct at press time, the author and publisher do not assume and hereby disclaim any liability to any party for any loss, damage, or disruption caused by errors or omissions, whether such errors or omissions result from negligence, accident, or any other cause.

Adherence to all applicable laws and regulations, including international, federal, state and local governing professional licensing, business practices, advertising, and all other aspects of doing business in the US, Canada, or any other jurisdiction is the sole responsibility of the reader and consumer.

Neither the author nor the publisher assumes any responsibility or liability whatsoever on behalf of the consumer or reader of this material. Any perceived slight of any individual or organization is purely unintentional.

Neither the author nor the publisher can be held responsible for the use of the information provided within this book.

All scripture, unless otherwise specified, are taken from the *Holy Bible*, New Living Translation, copyright © 1996, 2004, 2015 by Tyndale House Foundation. Used by permission of Tyndale House Publishers, Inc., Carol Stream, Illinois 60188. All rights reserved.

Scripture marked ESV are taken from The Holy Bible, English Standard Version. ESV® Text Edition: 2016. Copyright © 2001 by Crossway Bibles, a publishing ministry of Good News Publishers.

Scripture marked NIV are taken from the Holy Bible, New International Version®, NIV® Copyright ©1973, 1978, 1984, 2011 by Biblica, Inc.® Used by permission. All rights reserved worldwide.

Scripture marked NKJV are taken from the New King James Version®. Copyright © 1982 by Thomas Nelson. Used by permission. All rights reserved.

For more information, email: info@AnchorandLightPress.com
ISBN: 979-8-9926337-2-6 - eBook
ISBN: 979-8-9926337-0-2 - Paperback
ISBN: 979-8-9926337-1-9 - Hardcover

*To my wife Sonia, whose steadfast faith in the Lord
And belief in me is a lamp to my feet and a light to my path.
And to my children, Essence, James, Dakota, & Daniel,
Thank you for your continuous inspiration and optimistic curiosity.*

ACKNOWLEDGEMENTS

First, God's generosity with His wisdom and grace cannot be overstated. Thank you, in the name of Jesus our Lord. Second only to Him is my wife Sonia, who planted the seed for this journey of both following God, pursuing the highest levels of education, and writing in general. Thank you for being my helpmeet for our family and fulfilling God's *Missio Dei*. My children are my biggest fans, and if they are all who ever clap, that is enough. Thank you!

Pastor Steve Stells, founder of House of Prayer, now called Hope Point Church, has taught me so much about faith-filled leadership since my Christian infancy. Today, under your son Jonathan's leadership, a multitude more have the same opportunities to learn to walk as a disciple of Jesus, based on sound Biblical doctrine. Thank you both! Buddy Childress, founder of Needle's Eye Ministries, in the words of Steve Stells, you remain "a pillar in the faith community" for the Greater Richmond region. I can attest that you set the bar high for us marketplace ministry leaders, thank you sir!

And my friend and mentor in the national Christian writing and speaking scene, Carol Kent, founder of SpeakUp Ministries, one cannot codify the impact your dedication to the Lord's call in the face of overwhelming adversity has made on me. Thank you for creating a place for us to realize and magnify God's gifts! Thank you to SpeakUp leaders Gene Kent and Bonnie Emmorey as well.

Dr. Ed Read, your quiet presence in one's life, and faithful stewardship of God's wisdom is an example for us all. Thank you for healing our veterans, enriching our community with thriving participants from The Journey Home transition program, and bringing such depth to our weekly Bible study.

Dan Henghan, C12 Forums Mid-Atlantic Chair, and my brother in Richmond's BaaM (Business as a Ministry) initiatives! Thank you for your encouragement, guidance and for leading the charge to bring C12 to the RVA community.

And especially Paul M. Neuberger. Brother, thank you for your efforts in following God to build such a powerful ministry! C-Suite for Christ set the stage for me writing this book, as my eyes were opened to an explosive international need for this project to be completed now. Your time and contribution to its excellence are priceless.

Thank you to Anchor & Light Press, the Brighter Level Marketing team and my publishing coach, Scott Allan. And a special note of gratitude to Lora Thorson Creative for their work in production and design.

There are so many others who fertilized the soil for this project as well–Mark Thomas, Bobby Ukrop, Eric Edwards, Perry Miller, David L. Robbins, and Bob Mooney have all provided friendship, guardrails, and mentorship that is treasured to me. Thank you all!

CONTENTS

FOREWORD	xi
AUTHOR'S NOTE	xvii

PART I: WINNING PROPER: WHAT IS WORLD-CLASS BUSINESS AND FAITH-DRIVEN LEADERSHIP?   **1**

CHAPTER 1:	Crushing *Your* Goals	3
CHAPTER 2:	Origins Of World Class Business	17
CHAPTER 3:	Bright Eyes	29
CHAPTER 4:	Faith-Driven Leadership	43

PART II: YOUR OBLIGATION TO EXECUTE: WHY FAITH-DRIVEN LEADERSHIP?   **63**

CHAPTER 5:	A Marriage Of Faith And Business	65
CHAPTER 6:	Why God's Blueprint: A Few Runaway Trains	79
CHAPTER 7:	Faith's Geopolitical Importance	99

**PART III: HOW TO, FOR YOU: BECOMING A
FAITH-DRIVEN LEADER** — **119**

CHAPTER 8:	Who's Really In Charge	121
CHAPTER 9:	Words And Rhythm	135
CHAPTER 10:	Vertical Alignment	145
CHAPTER 11:	Playing Well With Others	157
CHAPTER 12:	Your Most Important Contract	167
CHAPTER 13:	Love Your Neighbor	187
CHAPTER 14:	Speak Only Truth	203
CHAPTER 15:	Appreciate Your Resources	215

**PART IV: HOW TO, FOR YOUR TEAM:
LEAD OTHERS TO VICTORY** — **227**

CHAPTER 16:	God's Favorite KPIs: The Quantitative	229
CHAPTER 17:	God's Favorite KPIs: The Qualitative	245
CHAPTER 18:	Discipleship At Work: Your Life's Purpose	259
CONCLUSION:	Next Steps For Success	273
WORKS CONSULTED		281
NOTES		283

FOREWORD

> "For the Lord gives wisdom;
> from his mouth come knowledge and understanding."
> –Proverbs 1:7

Have you ever questioned "conventional wisdom?" If not, you should. We all should.

Be honest: We're familiar with conventional wisdom. It's practices or beliefs that supposedly define things we should or shouldn't do.

We accept them at face value, as tried-and-true principles. Supposedly these notions are well thought out, and able to withstand intellectual rigor.

Except… this is rarely the case. All too often, conventional "wisdom" is pushed upon us by self-serving elites with their own interests in mind. In reality, the emperor has no clothes.

Trust me, I know.

Having founded C-Suite for Christ (www.csuiteforchrist.com), an international ministry of Christian business executives, I've encountered the walls of conventional wisdom at every turn.

My life's work is to break down barriers—many built by conventional wisdom—that block our organization's mission to cover the world in Christ. We *will* fulfill the Great Commission (Matthew 28:16–20).

One of the most egregious myths of conventional wisdom is that we should separate our work life from our faith life. Oh, we know the usual excuses: We don't want to "offend" anyone or be viewed as "intolerant" of others' beliefs.

So, we acquiesce … when we should be *pushing back* against these alleged "truths!"

See, conventional wisdom focuses on negatives.

It's always about the dramatic ramifications if its strictures are *not* obeyed—as opposed to the good that could emerge if the "rules" were bent. For example: Will the world really end if we bring authenticity to the workplace, and share our beliefs?

The Great Commission instructs us to "make disciples of all nations." It's abundantly clear.

The directive doesn't allow for whether we have time, or are in the right mood, or feel it's safe to share Christ's teachings. If so, wouldn't it be called the Great Suggestion or the Great Recommendation?

No, we should evangelize regardless of the world's pushback. This means not just in church, but in our homes and, yes indeed, the *workplace*. We shouldn't wear masks or tiptoe around the edges to hide Who we serve.

Being your true authentic self—*everywhere*—creates a high-quality existence. Obeying Christ's guidance makes us better people *and* leaders. This is the essence of Jerry Howard's thoughts and instruction. He recognizes that Jesus is the world's greatest business coach *ever*—a tireless Advocate for leading with love, forgiveness, vision, and grace.

We are destined to do well by following Him.

Putting Christ's Teachings to "Work"

The challenge of bringing Christ into the workplace has always been the "how." At the risk of mimicking conventional wisdom, the consequences *can* be significant if not approached correctly.

Whose advice should you follow? Where do you turn?

You can speak with clergy or others close to Christ. You can attend Bible study or a faith-based fellowship group. Above all, seek counsel from those who have "walked the walk."

Jerry Howard certainly has.

He's a servant leader who's ventured outside the typical comfort zone. He's a successful entrepreneur who's bought and started numerous businesses. Jerry understands how to create entities that deliver value, and concurrently enrich others' lives.

Sacrifices? Jerry knows.

He served in the US Marines, putting his life on the line for causes he believed in. His sense of duty, for doing what's right, is unmistakable.

He tried and failed at several endeavors too. After leaving military service, Jerry made some poor life choices, headed down bad paths. A steely soldier and business mentality led him to course-correct. He U-turned and gave his life to Christ.

Everything changed.

A New Business Model —and Mission

Conventional wisdom follows society's blueprint. Read this book, and Jerry Howard will show you how to follow God's.

You can build a business that glorifies Jesus Christ. You can display the moral leadership that comes from the world's best business coach *ever*.

Know that this takes courage. Let's openly embrace Christ's ethics. Let's stop denying these values are Christ-centric. Let's put stock in the *Holy* Word, not the human.

Jerry validates all this with God's teachings. He shows how to stand on Scripture. He provides lessons in being a faith-driven leader.

Doing so requires a changed mindset. You're not in business just to turn a profit anymore. You're working for an eternal impact on customers, employees, vendors … anyone the organization engages. The business is now about *saving souls*.

Jerry's guidance hones your world view. He lays out clearly, concisely, and scientifically how to achieve business success—*God's way*.

Once you get there, you'll never go back.

As an international keynote speaker who advises audiences on how to be more fruitful in life, I teach others how to fish. The best leaders share this mindset.

Jerry does so exceptionally well. His spiritual GPS leads you through a clearly-defined roadmap. This book is an instruction manual for being a faith-driven leader who glorifies God. Follow its steps, and Christ's kingdom will soon come into view.

Turning Things Around to Achieve Christ's Triumph

I earlier used the phrase "cover the world in Christ." This is the mission of C-Suite for Christ, the organization I founded.

Achieving it requires us to push back against multiple forces of secular society, who have increasingly sought to marginalize Christians. The commitment is serious and real.

We didn't get here overnight. It's taken a while ... and just like turning a cruise ship around, we can't reverse it suddenly.

Follow Jerry's recommendations, though, and life *will* change for the better.

Use your time, talents—and yes, business—to glorify God. Shine His radiant light everywhere possible. Be the beacon that leads others to finding salvation in Jesus Christ.

I'm blessed to be on an amazing journey with Jerry Howard as my mentor and friend. Read this book, and you'll feel the same way.

More so, we're blessed to have you with us on Team Christ.

We'll show the world why conventional wisdom is rarely wise ... and, in the process, open many hearts to the one source of true wisdom, forgiveness, and hope that will never leave them.

Yours in Christ,

Paul M. Neuberger
Founder, C-Suite for Christ
pneuberger@csuiteforchrist.com

AUTHOR'S NOTE

As Christian business leaders, we have a higher standard, a two-edged sword in the fight to leave the world better than before. Our call is both an eternal obligation and one of the immediate. In the marketplace, behind enemy lines you might say, we are to glorify God by raising up disciples of Jesus while simultaneously operating at a world-class level—regardless of title or position. Today, more than ever, they are considered two distinct endeavors. In fact, effort toward our present goals have far superseded the eternal. American business has forgotten that pursuit of the infinite accomplishes the finite—and with far better results.

Christian business leaders should represent the pinnacle of success. Many of them do. In fact, they are not widely publicized *because* they make good decisions, thereby mitigating or eliminating juicy scandals. Good actors, proper conduct, and humility are not proclaimed by most media outlets. They are not the standard subject in movies, nor the hero in video games. Although not seen en masse, faith-driven leaders mediate millions of miracles you'll never read about. As followers of Jesus in the American marketplace, we are on the front line between right and wrong. If we choose to ignore God's great commission, we silently agree with the torment that follows.

Faith Driven Leadership: God's Blueprint for World Class Business will be a roller coaster on faith, leadership, and business! Together, we're going to climb mountains, traverse desolation, and move at the speed of light. Every once in a while, we will come to a screeching halt. The importance of faith-driven leadership requires that we stop. And think. To facilitate that effort, for individuals as well as groups, each chapter will conclude with questions appropriate for the boardroom or Bible study.

Business leaders and owners who want to establish a regular Bible study should consider this a perfect resource for doing so. Church and small group leaders can do the same. Senior pastors who want to lead and establish a culture of marketplace ministry in their congregations will find everything they need within these pages.

Together, we will negotiate through the what and the why initially, but most of our time is on the how, of both faith-driven leadership and world-class business. If it is not obvious from the title, our exploration will consistently intersect those concepts. To me, faith, leadership, and business are as inseparable as Father, Son, and Holy Spirit!

My intent is to start with the largest, most relevant, macro perspective possible, a look into what are world-class business and faith-driven leadership. They should be synonymous, but the last one hundred-plus years of decision-making has largely been based on intellect—in homes, businesses, and the government. Faith at work is often pigeonholed into super-spiritual, meditative moments, but God is one of precision, metrics, and quantified winning, and He was so long before the first American corporation was established.

Regarding our inalienable rights, what Jesus did was model the sovereignty of an individual to choose. America simply applied that premise to governance. If we do not continue to live that out, every day, particularly at work, it will be lost to us as individuals, the marketplace, and our nation's government.

For the purposes of this book, the term faith will refer to the Judeo-Christian interpretation and execution found in the Old and New Testaments of the Bible. Once we're firmly established in what faith-driven leadership and world-class business are, I am going to dive into some of the most controversial topics, which I call *runaway trains*. By design, I hope to incite a desire in every person working in the marketplace to stand up for their faith and all people, as Jesus did. We will also investigate the real impact in dollars and cents. That review will explain why we need faith-driven leadership.

There should never be a faith-driven leader who does not manage his or her operation, region, department, or team at a world-class level. The qualitative partnership of faith and leadership, the quantitative KPIs for world-class business, married with God's favorite KPIs, will be codified as well. In doing so, how to execute on these concepts will be revealed. Contracting our viewpoint to the most personal level, we will unpack scripture and God's blueprint for world-class decision-making.

We will learn how to manage any business or team with just seven strategic, yet critical, metrics. We will wrap up with discipleship at work, using Jesus' own process for recruiting His number one guy, Peter. This will illustrate how to leave a legacy of leadership for your organization and the kingdom of Heaven, simultaneously.

Furthermore, God teaches that a braid of three cords will not easily break. Our three are: being a faith-driven leader, operating world-class, and making a present and eternal difference, all accomplished simply by changing our micro, daily decisions. Not unlike humanity's tragic yet prophetic beginning in Genesis, every catastrophic outcome we witness today started with a small, minute decision that faith could have prevented.

As history has witnessed, particularly in our lifetime, faith's relevance in business has been reduced to a mere vapor. It's barely a lingering scent, albeit sweet to the senses, but from which most cannot ascertain the source. Through brief case studies, scripture, and my own personal and professional failures and successes, it will be made plain the root of that fragrance. Thus, we unequivocally prove that God's blueprint for operating world-class is supreme. What's more, neatly organized in the world's number one, best-selling book, it has been right under our nose all this time.

We've all heard you cannot kill an ideology. I believe that is because ideology is beyond the physical and psychological. Good or bad, ideology is spiritual. My intent is to revive Judeo-Christian ideology in business to such a degree that it once again becomes axiomatic, but without losing sight of the Source. With the help of the Holy Spirit, the fruit produced in its bearers' lives will overwhelm and eradicate the popularity of any alternative. Particularly for those dogmas grounded in feelings, not fact, or worse, those rooted in pure oppression, my hope is they return to the fringe.

Now, your part. Think of that opportunity you never seized. Think of that leap you never made or that risk you wished you'd taken. This is that moment. Whether you are a multinational CEO, line worker, street corner preacher, or simply curious as to why the marketplace gets so worked up about Christianity, open your heart and mind, if just a bit. Worst case scenario, you'll learn why Christians seem so weird.

C'mon, we worship a guy who traveled around the desert 2,000 years ago with His friends, then let the local authorities nail Him to a cross—even though He was innocent! What's strange about that?

AUTHOR'S NOTE

Seriously though, my hope is you make an intrepid impact on your family, your job, your business, and your life!

God's train is leaving the station. If you take only one thing away from this book, know this: you have but two options. You can stand there stagnant, idly watching it move away, wondering why you have this lingering aroma in your heart. Or, you can climb aboard and learn what the supreme God of the universe has planned for you. Jesus said, "follow me." His words still echo through eternity in the hearts of all believers. I know He's in your heart, too, whispering the same. I am boldly asking you now. Follow me, read, and execute what's in this book, and hang on tight!

Follow Jesus, Lead Others.
Jerry Howard,
Chesterfield VA, 2024

PART I

WINNING PROPER: WHAT IS WORLD-CLASS BUSINESS AND FAITH-DRIVEN LEADERSHIP?

> Therefore, since we are surrounded by such a huge crowd of witnesses to the life of faith, let us strip off every weight that slows us down, especially the sin that so easily trips us up. And let us run with endurance the race God has set before us.
> -Hebrews 12:1

CHAPTER 1
CRUSHING *YOUR* GOALS

> "To live your life without God is the most unproductive thing you can do."
> –Matt Perman

Winning. What is winning? A number of years ago, with youth disappearing in the rearview, I wanted to get back in shape. My goal wasn't just good fitness, rather I wanted to reclaim my level from active duty in the Marine Corps. I looked around Richmond, VA, and saw all these people running. They were slim and seemed to float just above the pavement when they ran. I remembered feeling that way in college and on active duty, gliding over the sand when stationed in the hot, Mojave Desert of Southern California. So, I ran.

I trained for and completed two half-marathons in the following nine months. I lost some weight, but I didn't get *slim*—and I never seemed to glide. I just got good at running with fat! Half-marathons are hard, nonetheless. My "finisher" medals still hang in my closet. I do cherish them to some degree.

Today, I run occasionally, no more than two or three miles, but mostly I enjoy rucking. If you are not familiar, rucking is walking quickly with weight on your back. In the Marines, we did lots of that, and we hated it equally. Despite having said goodbye to youth, I can ruck, and it keeps me slim—as slim as I will ever be, anyway.

What I learned about training and finishing the race was that I was not going to be first across the finish line, ever. There were three or four guys from Kenya who were better suited to that honor. They competed and won all across the country. They were created for that genetically, mentally, even geographically, given where they grew up. I had to recalibrate my perspective on winning. Therefore, my personal definition became, "winning is the external manifestation of internal effort." If you're thinking, "pretty nebulous, Jerry," I agree.

> **Winning is the external manifestation of internal effort**

Today, as much as any time in history, there are millions of books, classified formulas, and elixirs to ensure that you reach peak performance and maximum output! Crush *your* goals with our secret to perfection, for only $9.95 a month!

Do they work? I've not read them all, but many. And they all help *you* get where *you* are going. They do lack one thing. They encourage *you* to define victory. In the Kingdom of the Lord, defining victory is not part of our task set.

When I ran those half-marathons, I didn't show up on race day and define the terms. In the race of life, the Author of Life defines its parameters. The author of Hebrews, who many believe was Paul, Barnabas, or Timothy, under the guidance of the Holy Spirit writes:

> Therefore, since we are surrounded by such a huge crowd of witnesses to the life of faith, let us strip off every weight that slows us down, especially the sin that so easily trips us up. And let us run with endurance the race God has set before us. We do this by keeping our eyes on Jesus, THE CHAMPION who initiates and perfects our faith. Because of the joy awaiting him, he endured the cross, disregarding its shame. Now he is seated in the place of honor beside God's throne. (Heb 12:1–2, emphasis added)

Paul clearly reveals the focus and the definition of winning. God defines not only the goal but the prize. The *what*

> **In God's kingdom, defining victory is not part of our task set**

and the *why*. Winning is completing the race *God* set before us. We are finishers in victory, but we are not the hero. Our goals are not the purpose.

The fastest person racing in those marathons was the winner according to the race designer's parameters. However, I—and many others—played an important support role. We were finishers. Our friends and family created the party and attracted sponsors and the media. Without us, most people wouldn't dare to *try*.

I may not be like the Kenyan, but I definitely enjoyed crossing the finish line. I still appreciate the medals and the knowledge that I overcame every obstacle preventing me from training and finishing. Laziness, 4:30 a.m. wakeups, equipment costs, blisters, hot weather, cold weather, sleet, rain, and even snow—the list of challenges was endless! Different from the first race in an urban setting, my second race was in a state park with lots of hills. Due to scenery and experience, I actually finished that one fifteen minutes faster!

God asks for the same participation in his half and full marathons. Jesus is the winner; our goals do not supersede His. We get to be a finisher in His kingdom. This is the highest honor. We are brothers and sisters reborn with Him. Not before Him, but equally counted as righteous. Since nothing that was made was made without Him, climb aboard! His race, which through faith we are guaranteed to finish, will be more adventurous, challenging, and delightful than anything you and I can fathom!

Looking at the world, who is winning? Is America winning? Is the marketplace winning? The church? Family?

The answers are absolute. *No.*

What happened?

> **A victorious mindset produces the discipline needed to push toward excellence, long after motivation has evaporated**

For most of our lives, we've all heard that winning isn't everything. We've heard, it's how you play the game. Playing the game correctly is important, but winning has equal value.

How would my Kenyan race colleague feel if I were on the podium with him despite finishing an hour later?

Knowing the techniques and rules and following them will facilitate a proper relationship between participants, but victory has to remain a focus. Simply learning the rules does not achieve an outcome worth the work. A victorious mindset, however, produces the discipline needed to push toward excellence, long after motivation has evaporated. The world, America, business, church, and family have all failed to meet the mark. Rather than dig in and exceed standards, every aforementioned sector has simply lowered them.

If you are interested in crushing your personal and professional goals to experience just a sliver of the diminishing American dream, I'm with you.

In fact, I'm sure you are thinking, "Yes, Jerry. Those things are important, but I have to pay my bills and feed my family. I want a better standard of living for me, my family, and my employees."

I want that too. Through countless personal and professional challenges, I have realized one thing about myself: I will stop at nothing to realize the vision that God put on my heart. Somehow, I got it in my spirit and soul that I could have the American dream. I could have my cake and eat it too.

I must be crazy to think that I could be good with God and successful in life, right?

What about you? Are you willing to take the mental and spiritual beating it takes to operate your life without fear, confusion, and lack of standard? Or are you going to achieve your goals through lies, manipulation, and complete self-interest? Even if you are doing it for your family, its still the wrong thing for the right reasons. Where's the standard in that?

That kind of thinking is what got us here. Despite the tone, I'm not judging. I've been there and done that—for most of my life! Before learning

> **One desperate prayer provided the nudge for massive change**

to operate by faith, I cut all kinds of corners, told countless lies to my friends and family, at home and the workplace. When making decisions about how to raise my kids, I tried to be the "best Dad" rather than do what's best for them.

There came a time when that pushed me so far down into a pit of despair I couldn't leave my own house. Externally, you may have been fooled. At the same time, I had a wife who loved me, two beautiful children, an MBA, and a successful Marine Corps background.

I almost lost it. I let the fear of not achieving propel me into a habit of ego-driven decision-making and excessive drinking. Working twelve-hour days and Saturdays, I hit the bar until the wee-hours after work, rather than go home.

Maybe you are not like me, so freakin' hard-headed that it takes multiple arrests and jail to change your purpose and direction. Yes, you read that correctly. The Marine, MBA, family man found himself in jail, yet again, for more than an overnighter. I'll cover more on that later.

> **More than a metaphor, fruit of the tree, good or bad, is a universal principle of human interaction written into the fabric of our lives by the Creator himself**

One desperate prayer provided the nudge for massive change. In just a few short months, I made a shift of my priorities. When you reorder your life to faith, family, then finances, love becomes your motivation, not whatever external image you are trying to uphold. When faith guides your decisions, the benefit of others becomes the fruit in your life. Your family, professional team, and your community improve—almost as if there's a pre-ordained path through the chaos, arranged just for you. Whenever I see bad fruit manifest, which is often faster than good, my ego is certain to blame.

Will I point the finger at the serpent? Do I blame my wife? Do I blame God?

Not anymore.

The free-market economy operates the same way. When leaders make decisions based on faith, the rising tide helps everyone improve. Conversely, when the hard truth is re-written or bad actors covered up, bad fruit manifests. The fruit of the tree—good or bad—is more than just a metaphor, it is a universal principle of human interaction written into the fabric of our lives by the Creator himself.

When an investor scouts a great idea and stakes an interest in an enthusiastic entrepreneur, she is saying, "Be bold. Do great things. I believe in you!"

When a factory line supervisor approves the promotion of a young leader, he says the same thing, "Be bold. Do great things. I believe in you!"

Thus, the invisible hand of faith-driven leadership manifests opportunities for everyone.

When was the last time someone said that to you? When was the last time we generally had emotional safety at work?

Faith driven leadership is based on principles that govern all people. They apply to everyone, not just followers of the way of Jesus. Business owners and executives are the front line for encouragement, ethics, and standards—in every sector in the country. Our leadership controls all the jobs in America. Our standards affect the lives of our employees and partners. Our taxes and lobbying dollars control the country's economic, and especially foreign policies.

Being world-class is more than just revenue and profit. If we are body, soul, and spirit, then so are our organizations, departments, and teams. Winning is succeeding in all three. Faith in a cause greater than ourselves is the only path toward a better future. Every decision, every day, leaders must fight the battle in our souls by casting aside thoughts of comparison and envy. We must vigorously pursue God's unique plan and purpose and persevere to its manifestation in our lives.

For example, Jesus personally wanted to heal His sick friend Lazarus, yet He stayed on God's mission. As a result, His friend died. How tragic.

Subsequently, at Lazarus's resurrection, hundreds of people believed in Jesus as the Messiah. Later, even He prayed for the cup of the cross to pass, yet He stayed on mission. His persistence has enabled billions of people to make Him Lord and now devote their lives to worship God and care for others.

Your soul is the battleground, but your family, business, career, or job reveals the fruit of your effort. As I said, winning is the external manifestation of internal effort.

"Okay Jerry, but how does all this spiritual talk affect my P&L statement? How am I going to get that bonus if I help John in marketing finish his project first? How can I worship a God who won't fix my car so I can get to work?"

Glad you asked.

Here's a quick spiritual example of massive wealth production. As a Christ follower, I believe Jesus operated perfectly under God's blueprint for world-class business. In fact, Jesus stated, "...I must be about my Father's *business*" (Luke 2:49b NKJV, emphasis added). He took five fish, thanked God with true gratitude in His heart, and shared with His friends. They, out of faithful obedience, passed around the baskets and fed 5,000 people. Jesus did this multiple times, all over town! You need only look around, do some Google searches, and you'll see the same blueprint at work.

I have a friend and brother in Christ who epitomizes a faith-driven leader. Not only that, but he has successfully executed on Jesus' aforementioned model for world-class business. Due to national security, he has chosen to maintain anonymity, but his story is no less compelling.

My friend's youth was spent knowing God, but letting the world grab a hold of his heart and mind at times, leading him astray. Later, with a reorientation toward the Lord, some great mentors, and sheer grit, he obtained his PhD and completed medical school to become an MD. He volunteers as a paramedic with a local volunteer rescue squad and travels to Third World countries on medical mission trips;

a great example of maximizing one's potential. He's also a Christian family man.

Initially, he and his brother, who struggled with life-long food allergies, founded and grew a pharmaceutical company. Its focus was building life-saving medicines for patients like them. Ultimately, they sold it for several hundred million dollars. Good fruit, but it gets better.

After succeeding with his first start-up, my friend founded an impact-driven pharmaceutical company. He knew it was not going to be a highly profitable business model at the time. He didn't care. He passionately pursued a righteous endeavor, leveraging his own financial resources from his first exit to drive forward a plan to help millions of patients, including children, who are impacted by drug shortages.

The company was founded in 2019 with a vision to fill a serious gap in America's medicine supply chain. Its primary goal is to provide basic, critical drugs that have been in shortage for our hospitals. It will provide stability to the essential medicine supply chain, beginning with the most important components, the pharmaceutical ingredients.

Less than a year into operation, the world shut down; not exactly a good sign for this new startup. China was finally revealed as a threat due to its production of the Covid virus. Ports were closed, and drug supplies were vanishing. At that time, China manufactured the vast majority of these important drug ingredients. This tiny little startup was now really important to national security.

In a matter of months, this "unprofitable" business model fed the multitudes. The company applied for, and received, an initial federal contract for close to a billion dollars to reshore our nation's essential medicine development and manufacturing industrial base.

My friend sacrificed part of his wealth, his five fish you might say. His worthy cause focused on building a company to secure drug manufacturing on US soil after the industry had moved abroad due to challenging economic policy. Bringing generic ingredient manufacturing back to US soil didn't exactly meet the world's criteria for a sound business model. The investment thesis, from an EBITDA and cash flow perspective, was also *not* textbook.

Nevertheless, he knew it was the right action for America. He knew God would see them through, not only getting his company built, but working toward sustaining it and turning it into something much bigger. With a servant-leadership mindset, this faith-driven founder was justified by God and led by the Holy Spirit to do good in this world. My friend showed up strong, made sound, biblically-based daily decisions to help others, and is letting God do the rest!

From his educational acumen and business savvy, one can easily conclude he was given the five talents from Jesus' parable. I like to think Tim and Demi-Leigh Tebow are of the same talent level. That might not be you. I was perhaps given two or three, maybe you were given only one talent. The point is not what you have, but what you do with it. My friend took a few hundred million and unselfishly worked toward billions. God wants you to multiply and produce fruit. From Genesis until now, that has not changed.

"Jerry, what about my goals?"

Crushing *your* goals is not winning. But there are objectives to accomplish. Think of it like this. True winning is planting a tree under whose shade you will never rest. This country was founded on thinkers like that. The Founding Fathers were statesmen, business owners, and family men. They did not get there alone, either. Countless men and families gave up their fortunes, or large parts of it, for the nation's independence—all to plant a tree we now enjoy. Most of us will never know their names.

God in heaven and every person who has heard the Gospel of Jesus as a result of American influence around the world will celebrate them in the next life. As a leader in business, that is you. That is me. That is our mission. Maybe not explicitly written in the Gospels, but our daily decisions echo in eternity. World class business enriched with faith-driven leadership is the key to preserving the sacrificial investment of both Jesus and the Founding Fathers. Every time we honor God with the time, skills, and fiscal blessings He gave us, we are playing our part to set the captives free!

Being a faith-driven leader has allowed me to lead executive teams to success and carried me through the darkest valleys of business failure.

> **World class business enriched with faith-driven leadership preserves the sacrificial investment of Jesus and the founding fathers**

Despite being in my early 30s, and only two years into my walk with the Lord, God's word gave me supernatural, unearned discernment in my first healthcare executive roles. His truth instilled in me fortitude to make decisions that were right and in accordance with policy but were hard and unpopular. Ninety percent of my direct reports were ten to twenty years my senior and had decades more experience. The pressure was immense. Yet, under God's grace, patients were healed, and profit manifested.

I've purchased businesses and scaled them with growth and acquisition strategies. I even shut one down and led a team through the daily uncertainty of reorganization. I've let God lead me to success and then cut right in front of Him, always to my detriment. Increasing revenue is one thing, and often easy, but implementing business systems takes more than just great ideas. That takes work and discipline. God's daily decision-making process has allowed me to buy back countless hours wasted on pursuing goals that were never His. My plan is to help you avoid learning the hard way.

Following God's blueprint has created a quality of life I only dreamed of when I first joined His family. Today, I get to speak to audiences and consult for business leaders across the country. Yet, I still pick my younger kids up from school three to four days a week. Occasionally, I have lunch with my older two in college, during the week! I occasionally coach sports and cook lunch after church on Sundays. At the time of this writing, I'm a full-time doctoral student in industrial and organizational psychology at Liberty University. Yet, I'm present with my family and leading others toward the future. This is God's plan for me.

What does your dream look like? What life is God building for you?

In the following narrative, we will uncover more of the what and why of faith-driven leadership. We will explore God's word, learn His blueprint for winning and operating a world-class business, department, or team. You will finally know how God's word and guidance guarantee victory in business, life, and eternity.

There is a cost, however. God is clear in Deuteronomy 29:29:

> The Lord our God has secrets known to no one. We are not accountable for them, but *we and our children are accountable forever for all that he has revealed to us*, so that we may obey all the terms of these instructions. (emphasis added)

If God gives you insight or revelation, you are required to act upon it, zero hesitation. Even clarity is not required, so it may feel foggy or uncomfortable. Reference Abram when God told him to "go" (Gen. 12:1) and only told him the destination *after* he left!

What is the cost?

Give up control. Give up your cares. I'm not encouraging you to become completely irresponsible; quite the opposite. Seeking God is the first step to abolishing *ongoing* worry (there will still be moments) and despair from your life. Here's how.

First, accept Jesus the Christ as your personal Savior and follow Him as Lord. If you've never overtly committed to Him with a prayer, now is the time! Say this prayer out loud:

> *Heavenly Father, please hear my cry for help and reveal Your Son to me. I am lost and I am a sinner. I need you. Please come into my heart and live with me. I want You as my Savior and I will follow You as Lord. Take over my life and make it Yours. I will remain with You all my days. Thank you. In Jesus name, Amen.*

Now it must be said ... Welcome to the family!

I am so glad you are walking with the Lord and with me, not only in this life, but the next. Your immediate next step is to join us online at the Jerry Howard International Community. The direct link is: https://jerryhowardinternationalcommunity.com/home

Enter your name and email address and let us know you just read this page and started or recommitted to walking with Jesus. Following that, plug into a local church and get baptized. Chances are, someone in your local area has already invited you and cannot wait to hear the news!

Finally, if God reveals anything, especially that which is *only* for you, then you and your posterity are required to execute upon that knowledge. So, teach your kids! Although He's the Creator and doesn't have to do anything for us, He never makes a request without a reward. He guarantees that you, your family, your team, and community will experience a blessing for a thousand generations. If you are ready to go all in on being a faith-driven leader and implementing God's blueprint for world-class business in your life, then fasten your proverbial seatbelt and keep turning the pages!

The Boardroom or Bible Study

For group discussion and individual journaling:

When has your internal effort manifested victory in your life?

When has defining your version of winning failed you? When have God's goals surprised you?

When has motivation failed you? Did you engage in discipline to overcome? Why or why not?

What desperate prayers have led to massive change in your life?

What instances in your life have revealed to you the truth of "the fruit of the tree?"

How have you witnessed business leaders trade metrics for honoring God? How did you feel? What action did you take? Why or why not?

CHAPTER 2

ORIGINS OF WORLD CLASS BUSINESS

> "All humans are entrepreneurs, not because they should start companies but because the will to create is encoded in human DNA."
> –Reid Hoffman

Business in any nation is largely a product of its customs and laws. Since its inception in 1789, American business and economic growth was a function of the freedom of movement of wealth and capital. It is not surprising that the essential abolishment of human totalitarian rule gave individuals the very freedom that God ordained from the beginning. America's prosperity has been the awe of many world leaders for hundreds of years. Less than fifty years from our Declaration of Independence, Lord Liverpool, British Prime Minister, not only describes, but incidentally prophesied over the United States in 1821 by stating:

> America has increased in wealth, in commerce, in arts, in population, in strength more rapidly than any nation ever before increased in the history of the world. (Sylla & Wright, 2013)

Please note the date. The year 1821 was less than a decade after the War of 1812, also known as the final wrap up to the Revolutionary War. There would have been no reason for the British Prime Minister to compliment the US, unless what he said was overwhelmingly true.

Until January 1, 1983, British citizens were still subjects of the Queen, although the monarch's power had been limited for quite some time. Yet, if goods and services needed to be appropriated, there was no argument. Conversely, in the US, government could not interrupt the freedom of exchange of ideas and capital unless for a good reason. Eminent domain must also be appropriately adjudicated. This was a profound shift in the mindset of governance and drove exponential results.

A closer look at this economic freedom is revealed by scholars Richard Sylla and Robert Wright who assert:

> Between 1790 and 1860, US state governments chartered 22,419 businesses, with minimum authorised capital totaling $4.58 billion, by special statute. The US, in both total and per capita terms, had considerably more corporations and authorised corporate capital than the UK, France or Prussia did over that same span. Differences in incorporation and capitalisation rates between nations were largely a function of differences in laws and politics, but differences among American states resulted more from differences in the timing and character of economic development. (2013)

The two scholars go on to detail further:

Our data show that the period from 1790 to 1860 marked a rapid increase in corporation formation. Few corporations were created before 1790—a handful in the colonial period and 20 to 30 in the 1780s. Chartering rose roughly ten-fold in the 1790s, when states incorporated 247 businesses. By 1860, state legislatures had chartered more than 22,000 additional business corporations, and some 4000 more—a yet incomplete count–formed under general incorporation statutes. ... In other words, the number of active US corporations probably increased ten-fold or more between 1860 and 1916. (2013)

To summarize, in a little more than a century, 1790 to 1916, hundreds of thousands of businesses had been chartered. Thus, they could barter and trade with one another, thereby multiplying the value of their resources with a level of synergy never before seen in world history. Freedom in one nation, under God, distributed wealth naturally and spiritually, with no central planning or social engineering.

In the case of Solomon, the Bible's number one Jewish king, Israel was still subject to his shortcomings. When both he and David got off track, the citizens suffered greatly. Elected officials in the US and business leaders can have a similar impact, but because most wealth is not singularly controlled, one person's mistakes get them voted out of office or fired. As a result, more than any other means, Americans have and continue to vote with their wallet.

Even the great King David surrendered to the worst levels of temptation, committing adultery and murder. God taught Moses the law and under the counsel of his father-in-law, Jethro, Moses delegated decision-making to tribal and local judges. This worked, but when the newly

> **I postulate America got closer to what God intended for human governance, and He blessed it**

established, post-Exodus Israel looked around, everyone else had a king and they didn't. America's democratic republic gets the closest to this original intent, plus with the added bonus of a Commander in Chief, a singular, yet elected representative to engage other rulers. America's Commander in Chief position is one of envy to the great Winston Churchill, arguably the world's most influential 19th century leader.

God never wanted His people to have a king. In great detail, He warned them of the coming misery (1 Sam. 8:10–22). I postulate that America got closer to what God intended for human governance, and He blessed it. Some may disagree, but hear me out. God is Judge, with a role similar to the US Supreme Court. Jesus is Chief Executive, not unlike the US President. And the Holy Spirit is the love and activity of Father and Son throughout the universe. Similarly, the US Congress represents the will of the collective population and their overall activity.

Countless judges and kings led Israel before Jesus' arrival, and after his ascension. And of course, He was never accepted by them as Messiah. But His message to the world remains clear. Human leaders, subject to immense temptation for corruption, must be a function of the people whom they serve.

Interestingly enough, countries whose origins were under British rule are still some of the most successful today. Their original intent was control of natural resources, not to establish thriving, independent countries. However, in the process of importing goods, Great Britain, more than any other colonial power, exported Protestant-Christian faith, parliamentary style governance, and incredibly high standards of conduct. Although America is largely known for its economic power and agility, Great Britain (in partnership with God's word, of course) gets much of the credit.

A dictatorial leader or group of leaders of any kind will ultimately succumb to the lust of power. Even benevolent dictators are soon replaced by evil ones. History has thousands of examples. In the wake of the 9/11 terrorist attacks, the executive branch of the US was greatly expanded. In the wrong hands, we've seen terrible misuse of power. In the kingdom of heaven, God "seated us with Him in the heavenly realms because we are united with Christ Jesus" (Eph. 2:6). Thus, we all report equally to our Lord.

The American founders knew this must be a staple component to proper governance. Most of them were faith-driven leaders. Not all of them practiced the same version of Christianity, or practiced at all. They were, however, well-educated, philosophical, and intellectual men who believed that Judeo-Christian values provided the bedrock for both proper governance and daily decision-making. Here are some of their thoughts. Washington in his farewell address states:

> Of all the dispositions and habits which lead to political prosperity, religion and morality are indispensable supports... And let us with caution indulge the supposition that morality can be maintained without religion. Whatever may be conceded to the influence of refined education on minds of peculiar structure, reason, and experience both forbid us to expect that national morality can prevail in exclusion of religious principle. (1796)

I will discuss this more later, but he is clearly foreshadowing the current state of US politics and business. His reference to "refined education" is what President Woodrow Wilson, Theodore Roosevelt, and many other founding Progressives supported as intellectual rule. They believed that more power in the hands of a ruling elite would increase their enlightenment and reduce the chance of corruption.

Yes. They actually believed that.

This supposition has eroded the bedrock of world-class business. That is, prosperity is a function of having a perfectly good, moral, actively involved, supernatural overseer under whom we must subject our evil actions. We must particularly subordinate those efforts that emerge, always from good intentions, to a higher ideal.

The result?

Humility.

Deists believe that God exists, but He does not interfere with daily human affairs, thus no miracles. Deism or otherwise, it's interesting to note that as these individuals aged, their belief in an uninvolved God seemed to have waned. An example is James Madison, who was reported to have been a deist, but toward the end of his life he wrote:

> Belief in a God All Powerful, wise, and good is so *essential to the moral order* of the World and to the happiness of man, that arguments which enforce it cannot be drawn from too many sources. (~late 1830s, emphasis added)

Many more of those who signed the founding documents were quoted to value Judeo-Christian principles. In fact, they were unanimously convinced that the American experiment could never sustain itself without moral leaders in business and politics.

But why do we care what they think, 250 years later? Who were they?

At the core, the founders were busy men, who did their best to provide for their families, both during their lives and posthumously. They cared about the day's affairs and the future. They were no different from the men and women of today, who work hard and give their best to those with whom they interact.

They were you. They were me. Just like they did, you and I have the ability to set a new standard in our homes, workplaces, and communities.

The Bible has numerous examples of those who reported directly to God and made a cultural impact. Solomon and David were already noted, and when properly subordinated to God, were great leaders. One of my favorites was Joseph from Genesis, his business acumen came directly from God and saved countless lives. Although subsequent Pharaohs' enslavement of the Hebrews brought about their downfall, while subordinated to God through Joseph's leadership, they were on top.

As with all humans, one person accountable only to themselves, controlling vast resources, always results in massive death and destruction. Free market business naturally curtails that tendency. Even CEOs and owners, through a matrixed environment, report to their customers. If the customers are not happy, they ultimately report front and center to a Board of Directors and shareholders.

World class business requires faith-driven leaders. The runaway trains described later are specific evidence of where intellect without morals has led. In his book, *Coming Apart*, Charles Murray attests that "only the virtues that made America great will continue to keep it great." Published in 2012, he reveals that in the last fifty years, 1960–2010, significant changes in the intellectual capital have coalesced into bubbles of "ruling elites" around five major centers of influence. Today, we are all too familiar with the Boston, New York, San Francisco, and Los Angeles regions' influence on national policy. The Washington, DC bubble is by far the most removed from reality. Increasingly, these individuals have more power than most, but have a decreasing belief in a power greater than themselves. Power corrupts.

> **Wealth naturally converges around people, services and products that bring the most value**

As noted above, different from any prior economic structure, the US was essentially a lack of structure. America's initial economic explosion resulted from millions of people working and controlling hundreds of thousands of businesses. Similarly, today's small and medium-sized business (SMB) consists of approximately one hundred million people controlling millions of businesses. These are a great example of the natural distribution of wealth. Accordingly, wealth converges around people, services, and products that bring the most value.

Conversely, the re-emergence of socialism should not be surprising. The belief is generally that a group of people with superior intelligence can appropriately engineer a society of perfect equity. Equity being the control of outcome. More later, but there is no possible process by which humans can control outcomes. Only extreme hubris could manifest the belief that outcomes for millions and billions of people can be controlled. However, it is the next logical conclusion from a ruling class in America. The prevailing thought process is basically, we're smarter, we know what is best, for you and everyone else. Friends, socialism is bad for business.

Take President Trump's 2016 presidential victory as a quick example. The belief that he could win was so far from the ruling elite's perception because the reality of most Americans' daily life was so far from their perception. Despite being a billionaire TV star, his appeal was that he didn't like what the ruling elites were doing to the country. Basically, he thought they were bad for business. Like him or not, do a video search of him from the 1980s through his first run for office, and today. He's been saying the same thing for almost fifty years. Most politicians would love that freedom of voice. I don't know his doctrine of theology, but faith-driven leaders, grounded in truth, never have to worry about saying the wrong thing.

Faith-driven leaders subordinate themselves to the same higher power, pray on their knees at the same altar, and worship from the same proverbial pews on Sunday morning as everyday people. Faith-driven leaders put others first while simultaneously working toward the common good, which includes them and their families.

Consider this for a moment. If you are a faith-driven leader currently suffering from burnout, I ask you this:

How many outcomes are you trying to control, more often described as, how many plates do you have spinning? How long have you spun them?

Two years is more than too much. I suspect some of you have been at it for twenty or more.

The ruling elite may have power and too much control, but they also suffer from monumental failures, most often highly publicized ones. Growing up, all I read or heard about in mainstream music was rap stars, their crew, and whatever new nickname they gave themselves that year. It was once reported that changing your nickname in music every year is good for sales. I guess. Today, the allegations against many of them are numerous and tragic. Why is this so common?

But Jerry, those are just personal issues people have, what do they have to do with economic policy and business metrics? Jay Clayton, former SEC Chair, appearing on CNBC, has stated on more than one occasion, but most recently on August 19, 2024:

> Economic growth comes from three things, energy cost reduction or production domestically, technological superiority, as the US develops technology and the world gets online, we all benefit, and last, capital allocation. We have four percent of the world's population, but fifty percent of its capital.

Our current national leaders, nearly all of those in government in the last twenty years, obviously have no knowledge of these facts. The words they use *seem* to affirm, but their voting habits and policy development consistently move us in the opposite direction. Not surprisingly, their problems are both public and mirror the stars in entertainment.

World business leaders invest where there is the greatest potential for return. Good, moral decision-making over the world's largest economy, upward of $29 trillion, and the US national budget which exceeds $6 trillion, is good for business. Even mediocre leaders who are predictable, and generally moral, increase world confidence and capital investment into the US.

We continue to outsource energy production and are increasingly mandating renewable energy sources that are known for inefficiency and natural habitat destruction. We have done nothing to prevent the Chinese Communist Party (CCP) from stealing intellectual property in the last thirty years. And many of our economic policy decisions are decreasing global investment in America while simultaneously reducing the perceived—and actual—stability of American currency.

Faith driven leaders in business would not have elected these individuals. Moreover, disciplined faith-driven leaders would not have supported these policies. American business has crept away from faith and is no longer world-class. The following chapters will reveal why faith-driven leaders are so important, but let's transition to a micro perspective of the mechanics inside world-class business.

The Boardroom or Bible Study

For group discussion and individual journaling:

Where has America gotten off track with regard to Biblical values?

What can you do personally to help steer the ship?

Where have you witnessed wealth converge around something you thought was wrong?

Good or bad, did that product or service provide value? To whom?

What could you do personally to prevent value being added to bad actors?

CHAPTER 3

BRIGHT EYES

> "Many of life's failures are people who did not realize how close they were to success when they gave up."
> –Thomas Edison

For a little over thirty years, starting in the early nineties, I have worked in business. Maybe you once shared my first job title, or lack thereof, "miscellaneous labor" was all the check stub read. The minor exception began three months after the terrorist attacks on September 11, 2001, where I began work for five years as a United States Marine. I worked a commission-only sales job during the recession and recruited for a nationally known university.

In executive leadership, I've operated small hospitals, typically owned by middle market companies, but each location was a singular business unit, or profit center. Most employed one to two hundred individuals and served 100–150 patients. My personally-owned companies never exceeded thirty full-time equivalents (FTEs). All that to say, I'm well-versed in the SMB (small and medium-sized businesses).

According to the Small Business Administration, most people in America, over 61 million, are employed by a small business. This is almost half of the entire workforce. 99.9% of all businesses are considered small. Eighty percent of those are solo ventures; meaning they have one owner and operator. The SMB greatly contributes to America's economic stability, and thus is the focus of this book.

Any business owner will tell you that hundreds or thousands of low paying customers is far more secure than a few large ones. Protecting small business protects America.

> **Protecting small business, protects America**

My friend Peter C. Fuller, author of *World-Class Speed: The Proven KPI-Based Structure to Accelerate Business Growth*, asserts that most people in small business believe they cannot operate with world-class standards. Here's what he says:

> 100% of the business owners I've surveyed will pick a Fortune 100 company as an example of a world-class operation. None have picked their own company or even a smaller business in their orbit. That's a sad statistic, considering most employees in the United States and the global economy work for small business owners. It's also sad given the tremendous benefits of operating as a world-class company. (2024)

What is a world-class company?

A world-class company has three main characteristics. First and most important, the CEO, owner, or primary leader (L1) has to be healthy, in body, mind, and spirit. Physically, there can't be any major diseases or illnesses impacting decision-making.

How do we know?

Think of your current or last boss or the company owner. Mentally, are they someone you want to be around? Spiritually, do they submit to a power or authority greater than themselves?

They can be amidst challenge, but not in a state of desperation. He or she is challenged in healthy ways, relying on their faith, serving their family, and effectively managing all their finances. It's important to note, there will always be times of feast and famine, but how do they handle themselves?

The second component is happy stakeholders. Stakeholders are the executive or leadership team (L2), the employees, the customers, and, if any, the shareholders. "Happy," I know, is a very loose word.

What does "happy" look like?

Happy is yes to these questions: Do the leaders and employees truly work toward the good of the company? Are they getting what they deserve according to market standards? Are the customers' and shareholders' expectations being met? Are they in a positive disposition toward the organization?

These first two may seem very qualitative, but each can be thoroughly measured and tracked. Many consulting companies, including my team, called *iNTREPiD iMPACT Team*, have assessments and software that can easily evaluate where the leader and stakeholders stand.

The last component of a world-class operation is it must be an industry or sector leader in some way, not just meeting industry standards, or making money, as many in small business like to tout.

What are the criteria?

In what metrics do they lead the industry? Would someone purchase the company? For how much? The simplest valuation is what kind of multiplier can you get for income and owner's discretionary. Even better, what is the valuation as determined by an outside firm?

An external valuation is a good investment at any time. It can determine not only the company's immediate monetary value, but most importantly, its *potential*. Potential not only predicts the company's future, but its impact in the community, the market, or perhaps the world. Later in the book, specific KPIs will be detailed to aid this pursuit.

World-class businesses are healthy, happy and have value. They are owned and run by world-class people. Ideally, the L1 leader (CEO or owner) is multiplying his or her healthy behavior down through the leadership and into the employees, customers, and stakeholders.

One of my favorite world-class people is someone we will call, John Cartwright. Many years ago, I was hired into his emerging leaders program to learn to run post-acute hospitals. He was the first who modeled and taught me how to multiply healthy leadership. As the COO of the company, our first meeting was my final interview before entering the executive training program. It went something like this.

After giving some background, I was asked a series of questions unlike those of any interview I'd experienced before.

"Tell me about a time when you were asked to take a leadership role, but had little to no experience or foreknowledge." Cartwright requested.

I thought about college. I thought of the Marines. Jail flashed through my mind. But I was a different person now.

What *have* I done?

I thought of staying at home with the kids. Then it hit me. The first time I coached youth sports had only been a few months prior to this.

"What comes to mind, sir, is coaching *Upward* basketball," I started.

"Go on."

"Well, I played baseball—many years of it—but my son doesn't like it. I'm okay with that, but he wants me to be a coach, and he wants to play basketball. My wife and I encourage them to try all the sports, so I signed up to be an assistant coach."

"I coached soccer for my daughter. How old is your son?" Cartwright asked.

"He's six." I continued, "When the email came as to what my assigned team was, the church director noted at the end, 'And we've got a great assistant coach picked out for you as well.'"

"Didn't you say you signed up for that?" Cartwright was sharp. "That's right. I was sure there was a mistake. I'd never played organized basketball and never coached anything, even baseball at that point, either. I emailed him asking if he made a mistake. His response was, 'we're short on head coaches, Jerry, but you're a Marine, you'll figure it out,' followed by a winking smile in big font. He knew he had me dead to rights. As a Marine, there was no way I was going to whine my way out of that, so I did what all Marines do."

Cartwright laughed and leaned back in his chair. "Improvise, adapt, and overcome!"

"You got it, sir!"

"So, how'd the season go?"

"It was a rocky start; we lost our first two games. Five and six-year-olds are fun, but at any moment, one of them might grab the ball and go hide under the chair! In a game! You just never know."

Laughing, he asked, "How did you adapt?"

"We abandoned all hope of dribbling."

"That's hilarious!" Cartwright relaxed further.

"I just taught them how to pass really, really well. Two of the kids could shoot decent enough so we finished the season 12-2 plus came in second for the league in the playoffs."

"What fun, what fun." Cartwright sat up and looked at his watch. "Mr. Howard, those were all the questions I had, what do you have for us?"

Needless to say, I got the job. A few weeks after I started, Mr. Cartwright, who often taught his forty or so executive administrators personally, was teaching all the current operators and trainees about how to hire excellent leaders. He went through the normal, behavior-based questions he asked all of us. Although there are hundreds, he stuck with ten total.

Cartwright taught us most people beat around the bush, are not specific, or sometimes just ramble without answering the question. If they actually answer the question, and give a specific example, the applicants get a one. If not, they get a zero. That's it. If they get eight points or more, then he only looks for one other thing.

He said there is a qualitative element to the hiring process. He looks for "bright eyes." He said bright eyes are what heals patients—even when they're dying—bright eyes calm families and inspire teams to push through all their drama and nonsense. In an industry with such slim margins, high turnover, and unfortunately death, they refused to have anyone that lacked bright eyes leading their businesses. He concluded the training by saying, "None of you would be in this room if you didn't have 'bright eyes' when we met."

No one since has taught me anything so simple, yet so rich with revelation. If there was an $E=MC^2$ for talent acquisition, it would be "look for bright eyes." I do not recall him referencing scripture in his teachings, but I learned that God ordained "bright eyes."

> **If there were an $E=MC^2$ for talent acquisition, it would be, "look for bright eyes"**

In fact, Isaiah's book reveals why hiring bright eyes is important. He writes:

> Your eyes will shine, and your heart will thrill with joy, for merchants from around the world will come to you. They will bring you the wealth of many lands. (Isa. 60:5)

Breaking this down a bit, everything that a thriving hospital, or any organization needs is clearly illustrated. A joyful heart is the brightest light in acute and post-acute care. It truly does "heal the nations" (Rev. 22:2). Merchants here can be business owners, and especially, tradespeople. Healthcare practitioners of all types are among today's artisans. Wealth is not just financial. The "wealth of many lands" is experience. What we learn from Isaiah, thousands of years before human resources were a thing, is that bright eyes bring joyful hearts and a wealth of experience.

Nothing on earth influences others more effectively than a faith-driven leader. Bright eyes do not require Christianity, but one who operates at the intersection of faith, leadership, and business certainly possesses them. Reference Figure 1.

Figure 1

Faith, Leadership & Business are as inseparable as Father, Son & Holy Spirit

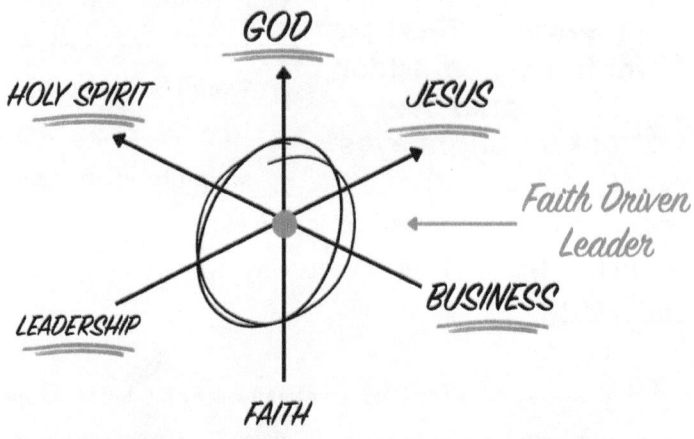

Note. Our faith points to God, our leader is Jesus, and free market interactions are guided by the Holy Spirit.

Mr. Cartwright is a faith-driven leader and a world-class business person. He's a fighter and has a reputation of working through and overcoming some of the most detrimental union takeovers of healthcare centers. I'm not for or against unions, but the second-hand accounts I've gotten have never been five-star. Modeling his behavior earned me the reputation of being a turn-around executive as well. That training and experience catalyzed my consulting organization today.

Cartwright also taught us the dangers of hiring second-rate leaders and those that *lacked* bright eyes. To paraphrase what he used to say:

> First-rate players always hire first-rate players. And if you are not sure what you are, then it will take great courage to overcome your insecurity when hiring your L2 leaders. The best people for the job need to have 'bright eyes,' and may intimidate you a bit. Your bright eyes attract great people, as long as you can lean into others' strengths rather than compete with them.

It's not unlike the military. Until you make Major, pay grade O-4 and above, young officers are always responsible for leading senior enlisted, who are very specialized. Similarly, our directors and senior leaders were highly experienced, often with lots of education. They oversaw only one aspect of the operation. Administrators, not unlike officers, are *master generalists*.

He taught that if we hire someone whose knowledge, skills and ability doesn't *exceed* our own, it only gets worse. Yes, you read correct. First-rate players need to be better than you in some areas, in order to compliment you.

As we move down the chain of command, second-rate players don't hire first or second-rate players, they hire third-rate players. Third-rate players hire fifth-rate, and fifth-rate players hire eighth-rate players.

By the time you make it from CEO to floor nurse or night shift supervisor, you are scraping the bottom of applicants. Integrity and work ethic do not appear in that subset. But first-rate players hire first-rate players, all the way down the line.

Do yourself a favor, be a first-rate player. If you don't think you are, just copy one. Do what they do.

It was a blessing to be mentored by someone so prominent in the field. He was the first executive level, faith-driven leader for whom I worked. His impact was nothing short of permanent. He was a world-class business operator and highly respected person.

Healthcare has many faith-driven leaders, so it was a great start to my executive experience.

Ultimately, I wanted to run my own calendar and build something on my own. Thus, I left the industry and bought a few businesses. That decision helped to finance the founding of *Jerry Howard International* and our consulting branch, *iNTREPiD iMPACT Team*.

If it weren't for first-rate leaders, as Mr. Cartwright affectionately coined, who to me are synonymous with world-class business people, I would be divorced, in jail, or dead. I would be filled with anger, cynicism, and hate. My immediate family would be half its size because my younger two children wouldn't exist! My extended family would be infinitely worse off and not following God.

Who gets the credit then?

Certainly not me—not the world-class business people who took me under their wing, either. The credit goes to Jesus Christ. Like most, I have moments of periodic depression. The enemy starts to kick at any of my top priorities—faith, family and finances. Our spiritual enemy wants to remind us of all the failures we've caused and how we are not good enough.

> **Humility is the foundation for world-class business and good moral decision-making**

He's right. Like it or not, thinking that I deserve any good thing is wrong. I don't. None of us do. Thinking the world owes you something is the fastest way to a prideful fall. Humility is the foundation for world-class business and good moral decision-making. People want to believe they are good, but we aren't. Jesus agrees:

> As Jesus was starting out on his way to Jerusalem, a man came running up to him, knelt down, and asked, "Good Teacher, what must I do to inherit

> eternal life?" "Why do you call me good?" Jesus asked. "*Only God is truly good.* But to answer your question, you know the commandments: 'You must not murder. You must not commit adultery. You must not steal. You must not testify falsely. You must not cheat anyone. Honor your father and mother.'" (Mark 10:17–19, emphasis added)

Jesus stopped there because he knew the rich young ruler could check those boxes. But he lacked submission to the first few commandments. He was unable to give up his earthly status.

> "Teacher," the man replied, "I've obeyed all these commandments since I was young." Looking at the man, Jesus felt genuine love for him. "There is still one thing you haven't done," he told him. "Go and sell all your possessions and give the money to the poor, and you will have treasure in heaven. Then come, follow me." At this the man's face fell, and he went away sad, for he had many possessions. Jesus looked around and said to his disciples, "How hard it is for the rich to enter the Kingdom of God!" This amazed them. But Jesus said again, "Dear children, it is very hard to enter the Kingdom of God. In fact, it is easier for a camel to go through the eye of a needle than for a rich person to enter the Kingdom of God!" The disciples were astounded. "Then who in the world can be saved?" they asked. Jesus looked at them intently and said, "Humanly speaking, it is impossible. But not with God. Everything is possible with God." (Mark 10:20-27)

There is much to glean from this passage. Most obvious is his inability to follow Jesus. He also never called Him Lord, only teacher, lacking the ability to fully submit in his heart.

The disciples were astounded, primarily because of culture. It was believed that rich people were more righteous because of their wealth. Jesus confounded them as well.

Like the rich young ruler, lack of humility in the marketplace today is the number one cause of its decay. This is not to say that we have to earn His grace, we can't do that either. Understand that by God's grace alone we get to learn, live out, and share His word. But what a privilege … What a privilege!

Humanity lacked any shred of humility until Jesus modeled it as a way to win. Humbling ourselves to God is winning. Becoming faith-driven, we acknowledge His goals are better than ours. Privileged in sharing the victory, let's refer back to Paul's perfect definition of winning:

> … let us run with endurance the race God has set before us. We do this by keeping our eyes on Jesus, the champion who initiates and perfects our faith… (Heb. 12:1b-2)

To win, we must seek eternal victory, not just physical or social. Good news to all of us ambitious business leaders, God's plans for you are far greater than you can imagine. Though we are not the apex hero, we still win!

How?

If the CEO directed the chief operator to pursue a new market, he will certainly approve the resources needed. Thus, if God's vision for your life is the best, then you can expect to be abundantly equipped to get the job done. Pursue the Lord, and everything you need will show up at your doorstep. Check this out:

> So don't worry about these things, saying, 'What will we eat? What will we drink? What will we wear?' These things dominate the thoughts of unbelievers, but your heavenly Father already knows all your needs. Seek the Kingdom of God above all else, and live righteously, and he will give you everything you need. So don't worry about tomorrow, for

> tomorrow will bring its own worries. Today's trouble is enough for today.
> (Matt. 6:31-34)

God is specific here. Don't worry. Seek Him. Do the right thing. He will give you everything you need. Then again, don't worry. The process is perfectly book-ended with "don't worry."

Just like the rich young ruler, those of us who worry can never find peace. Worry will never allow us to lay our titles, wealth, or authority aside to follow Him. Try we must.

Easier said than done. How many plates did you say you were trying to spin? Are you trying to engineer a society of millions or billions of people? Or just 30 FTEs?

Humans—leaders—we need to quit fooling ourselves.

In America, leaders who truly operate with humility, that is, accept that they might actually be wrong, are world-class. Leaders who submit to a power and authority higher than their own are world-class. Leaders who seek to control only their attitudes and actions are world-class. Leaders who ensure that those actions improve the lives of themselves, their families, stakeholders, and communities are world-class. Friends, this is the origin of world-class business. Humility.

The Boardroom or Bible Study

For group discussion and individual journaling:

What can policy makers do to better protect small businesses and the middle class in America?

What have, or will you do, to operate as a faith-driven leader? How can you better integrate faith, leadership, and business?

Have you ever made a trust decision based on "bright eyes?" Why or why not?

How do you remain in a steady state of humility in your personal and work decisions?

CHAPTER 4

FAITH-DRIVEN LEADERSHIP

*"The greatest danger in times of turbulence is not the turbulence;
it is to act with yesterday's logic."*
–Peter Drucker

Do you wear different personalities at work and home? If you answered yes, this is not uncommon. Approximately twenty to thirty percent of my clients have tested differently on their digital personality assessment versus the one-to-one deep dive. On one hand, we may be acting how we think others want us to. In other cases, we may be responding as the situation demands. A righteous case for both can be made. Regardless, I find either to be mind-numbing and exhausting.

Not only is it tiring, but Christian leaders who allow their environment to dictate their actions, will fail to inspire others to excellence. To the unsaved, the Body of Christ looks as fractured as broken glass and inundated with multiple personality syndrome. As

Christ bearers, we are called to be a thermostat, not a thermometer. Since Jesus is the Cornerstone, He has established the plumb line on which our lives are to be aligned. No other standard should be revered. Here's what that looks like for us.

Jerry Howard International is the highly creative arm and represents the influencer part of our businesses. JHI makes a macro impact. My team and I make video content, write, and give speeches and interactive keynotes, particularly on how faith, leadership, and business intersect. I also write books.

iNTREPiD iMPACT Team consists of myself and other faith-filled team members who have vastly different skill sets. Each of us brings immense value to every organization with which we work. This is how we impact the world on a micro level, one company, team, family, or person at a time. The lowercase "i" reminds us that "it is not about me." I'm here to represent Him. Jesus gets the only capital "I."

Our newest program, *Executive Corps*, is a faith-driven business leader round table based on three concepts: Follow Jesus, Lead Others, Operate World-Class. Our groups, six to eight members each, use much of this material to achieve success in faith, leadership and business, from the Spirit, to strategy to the spreadsheet.

Personally, my best skills are twofold. I provide world-class leadership training in organizations of all sizes. This is the qualitative side of our offering. I equip business leaders and their teams with tools to maximize self-awareness and personal performance. In my coaching and training sessions, we uncover the most natural superpowers and blind spots that prevent clients from bringing their best.

Our outcomes ensure that teams enthusiastically show up and bring their best. According to most HR research, for every team member my clients do not have to replace, we have saved them twice the annual salary of that individual. Saving multiple mid-six figures for a mid-five figure investment is a no-brainer.

Quantitatively, typically in small to medium-sized companies (SMB), I teach leaders the KPIs on which to focus and those to delegate. Even a small amount of accountability here can improve metrics by two and three-digit percentages. Clients who are fully committed to change can reasonably expect improved performance in just two or three quarters.

More than anything, what sets us apart is faith. We align company KPIs with God's KPIs, a perfect blend of the art and science of world-class business.

The consulting industry is booming due to an overall lack of accountability in leadership. Leaders often have trouble seeing the forest for the trees, particularly if they started the company. Surprisingly, we've found the difference between owning your job and creating an asset is not well-known in the SMB community.

> **We've found the difference between owning your job and creating an asset is not well-known in the SMB community**

You may be thinking, "Great, Jerry, nice to know about your work, but what does this have to do with faith and business?"

You are right, it is a shameless plug for our team's efficacy. More importantly, in our creative output, there's faith, leadership, and business. In our leadership training, there's faith, leadership, and business. In our business consulting services, there's faith, leadership, and business. We are always us—at home, at work, and in the community. We walk out our faith and the leadership and business principles we teach.

We believe that faith, leadership, and business are as inseparable as Father, Son, and Holy Spirit. World-class business sits at that intersection. Any influencer from Steven Covey to John Maxwell to Simon Sinek will attest that leadership requires faith. It's probably obvious that business requires people, and without a doubt people require good, moral leadership. Figure 2 illustrates.

Figure 2

Faith, Leadership & Business are as inseparable as Father, Son & Holy Spirit

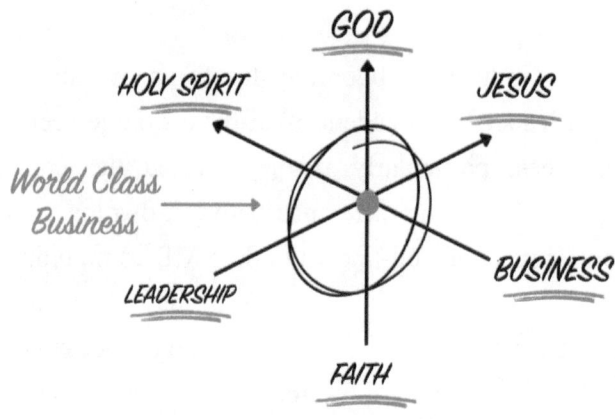

Note. World class business intersects similarly with faith-driven leaders.

Our processes and systems uncover the participant's most *natural* tendencies. These are the bread crumbs for what behaviors come from upbringing and training versus God-given talents. We reach back through one's story to uncover their best leadership skills—and God's call. Faith and leadership intersect here.

Once we reveal a leader's blind spots, and those of the team, we can appropriately arrange them to achieve the desired organizational outcomes. Leadership and business intersect here. Once the business is a well-oiled machine, CEOs will manage only the most strategic KPIs. True discipleship begins and leaders can multiply themselves, just as Jesus did. Business and faith intersect here.

> **Jesus spent the majority of his life as an entrepreneur**

And let's not forget, other than childhood, Jesus spent the majority of his life as an entrepreneur. From approximately twelve to thirty, he was a business owner, a carpenter to be exact. We in the marketplace have more in common with Him than you might think.

Want to guess whether He was world-class? Or faith-driven?

That's quite refreshing, isn't it?

Faith, leadership, and business aren't just abstract concepts that intersect in the marketplace; they deeply influence our personal journey as leaders. Understanding our God-given talents and embracing true discipleship can bring about profound change, not just in our organizations, but in our own lives as well.

When I embraced my faith, I began to see this transformation firsthand. Before answering Jesus's call, I was a chameleon at best. After submitting to Jesus as Lord, I had already suffered PTSD-like symptoms from pretending to be something I'm not for more than a decade. Most of my twenties were spent play-acting something you'd find in a B-rated gangster movie, at great personal expense. I ignored the moral framework I was raised with just to fit in with people who were going nowhere.

Here's a quick snapshot of how reporting to jail for the last time in my late-twenties felt and where I was before accepting God's grace.

Reporting time was 10 a.m. I was dropped off at 9:15 so she could get to work. No goodbye kiss. No word of encouragement. Did I hear the tires squeak just slightly as she pulled off? I wasn't sure the door was completely closed either. Not a glance in my direction. I was lucky she stayed true to her wedding vows, much less gave me a lift to the county jail. Which jail was worse, hers or the county's?

The air was thick with the droning hum of cicadas, a sound that always made my skin crawl. How could something so small produce such an overwhelming, unsettling noise? The humidity clung to me like a heavy blanket, making every breath feel like a struggle, as if I were suffocating beneath a plastic bag. The sight of the windowless jail only compounded my anxiety, its harsh, unbroken walls looming under the unforgiving August sun. With sunglasses forbidden inside the facility, the blinding light grew more oppressive with each passing moment, amplifying the unease settling in my chest.

Jail strips you of title, pride, and strength. Weakened more than spiritually, the outer door was heavy—a boring brown-on-brown frame and handle, probably the least expensive. No air conditioning in the foyer, the humidity hung worse here. At least I was out of the sun and my ears got some relief from nature.

No one chooses to be there so no need to watch the entrance, the reception window was empty. No shadows danced beyond the tinted glass. Only the most defeated, lowest flight risk were allowed the *privilege* of escorting themselves to jail. Was that a victory? Or an insult? Non-violent offenders were given the illusion of choice. What was winning for criminals? Not getting caught. If caught, being the worst of the worst. I failed at both.

My legs were mush. No chairs, no rest for the wicked. I leaned against the brown, cinder block wall and slid to the floor. Endless waiting ensued. What time was it? No watches or phones were allowed either. Could counting minutes make the time pass? The pressure on my heart teamed up with the humidity, amplifying the deafening silence.

My nerves overacted to the slightest noise, scratching the chalkboard in my head. It had been forty-plus days since my last drink. Surely, I've done a lot scarier things than this? Marine Corps Boot Camp, combat training. I had some college, officer candidate training, and high school JROTC. I always had some achievement to hide behind. Here, escorting myself to jail, I wasn't even winning in the criminal category.

My glittering image shattered; my proverbial high horse obliterated. How much time did I waste trying to be something I'm not? I can't remember what winning looks like.

Jail cells are a great example of rock bottom. I've been to plenty. That day, reporting for jail, I had no idea that in less than five years I would be CEO of a small hospital. Nothing short of miraculous, I am proof, when God has a job for you to do, you'll get there.

> **Reporting for jail, I had no idea that in less than five years I would be CEO of a small hospital**

I do not recommend trying to replicate my starting point. I suspect, however, that you've stagnated somewhere. Executives and founders stagnate just as bad as inmates.

Ever referenced jail when referring to your company? Or position? What about "golden handcuffs?"

Mine weren't golden, but yours may be harder to break. Deep down, we all want to know where we truly belong, not just family or job, but the big picture. God created us with that longing, so we would pursue Him.

My conversion was Providence because he was not a preacher. It was a businessman with an amazing testimony and a love for God, who gave the sermon and altar call that changed my life. He was not only under the lights of the stage, but his inner light radiated, and his words projected a rock-solid conviction about who he was and where he fit into God's kingdom. I wanted that, more than anything I'd ever wanted before in my life. It was the *one thing* I lacked.

Fast-forward a few years, I was in a meeting with one of the directors of rehab in a small post-acute center I operated. Somehow faith came up, and she remarked, "Well, I assume you are a Christian man, you have this light about you." I nonchalantly agreed and asked where she went to church. We discussed that for a few more minutes and ended the meeting.

On the drive home, lightning struck! I had become like Matt, the businessman on stage that day whose altar call I answered. My light, God's light, was radiating outward, and people noticed. Radiating light should be our goal, not to condone all things trendy today. We live according to the Bible. When we mess up, which is daily for me, we repent and change our attitude and actions. We don't change the truth to fit how we feel in the moment. We have an authority above us who makes the rules. We follow. The first and most consistent message Jesus delivered to His disciples was, "Follow me." It's a command, not a suggestion.

For example, when my team is contracted to deliver leadership training, it may not be appropriate to share the Gospel of Jesus or discuss Bible verses. So, we don't. Initially, in KPI training, Biblical discussions are rare. But at no point am I shy or restrained about revealing my faith. It's who *I am*. Jesus didn't always heal the sick, or convict the hypocrites, or feed the poor, but he always led the way. Faith-driven leadership embodies the same spirit.

Sometimes I even reference Paul from the New Testament in the boardroom. As a well-known figure from history, Paul is a great

> **We don't change the truth based on how we feel, we have an authority above who makes the rules, we follow Him**

example of a type of personality we reveal in leaders. If you are curious, Paul was likely an ENTJ (Extrovert-iNtuitive-Thinker-Judger) from the Myers-Briggs Type Indicator system, a super high D from Dominance Influence Steadiness Compliance or DISC system, or Pioneer Guardian in our system, called the 5 Voices created by GiANT Worldwide. By doing so, the participants learn two things: Jerry knows a bit of scripture, so he's probably a Believer, and Paul was a very precise, motivated, militaristic world changer. No one is offended. My faith is obvious, and I use it to lead the way.

Not long ago, I was asked to moderate a panel for a local Diversity, Equity, Inclusion, and Accessibility (DEI&A) symposium. This was initially quite the challenge for me. The stage consisted of multiple people with whom I disagree on foundational issues. I believed that from the stage, my questions and comments should include my worldview. To adequately prepare and in an effort to be thorough, I asked multiple groups in my personal network for suggestions. I got everything from DEI is destroying the country to dissertation-like statement questions with an agenda.

My closest friends knew my concern beforehand, though.

How was I, a Christian, going to moderate this panel effectively, without bias?

It's obvious where my personal beliefs lie. Personal feelings notwithstanding, I cannot deny my Lord in public.

How would I do this correctly?

My friend and colleague, Mark, stated it so plainly and perfectly. Sharper than any two-edged sword, he remarked, "Jerry, you need only be the Christ-bearer that you are." That's when it hit me. This has nothing to do with me. It's about Jesus. Luke records:

> I tell you the truth, *everyone who acknowledges me publicly here on earth, the Son of Man will also acknowledge in the presence of God's angels*. But anyone who denies me here on earth will be denied before God's angels. Anyone who speaks against the Son of Man can be forgiven, but anyone who blasphemes the Holy Spirit will not be forgiven. And when you are brought to trial in the synagogues and before rulers and authorities, don't worry about how to defend yourself or what to say, for *the Holy Spirit will teach you at that time what needs to be said*. (Luke 12:8–12, emphasis added)

What did I do?

First, I prayed for God to give me His agenda. Then I began researching the panelists. Through my research, I learned why the panelists teach in that industry. Depsite its dissonance with the 14th Amendment and the Civil Rights act of 1964, what I learned was that DEI&A had unfortunately been hijacked by thousands of ill-intentioned persons. This is why many organizations have spent millions, perhaps billions, with no effect. To my delight, none were on the panel. In fact, each of them revealed how they sought to overcome the stigma that the DEI&A space has come to bear. One panelist even shared my same faith!

My research revealed the questions most appropriate for this venue. I asked questions that revealed the strengths of the candidates. I asked them how they navigate the challenging and highly controversial perspectives some individuals hold as truth. I allowed them to describe how they approach organizations in a way that creates and fosters unity. Rather than push some agenda, I used my faith to find points of agreement with them and between them. Everyone's opinion and life experience brought value to the dialogue.

Was the first amendment hard at work?

It certainly was. The media and the woke left would have us believe otherwise. There are many who would do away with the first amendment in order to eliminate "misinformation" and "dangerous" questions. Do not let the television or social media define your truth. God defines truth.

Finally, in my prep to moderate, I remembered that free speech is a right of all Americans, and their opinions should be heard. The oath I took to support and defend the Constitution allows for and encourages disagreement. To my surprise and delight, there were many Christians in the audience as well. I was later approached with gratitude on how I represented the faith with compassion, yet was steadfast in its doctrine.

Now, more than ever, faith-driven leaders need to come together and be a light to which others are attracted. Our lifestyle choices, beliefs and doctrine should not change based on the new trends of the day. When we agree that truth is grounded in God's word, those principles remain effective.

> **Do not let television or social media define your truth. God defines truth**

Take the US Constitution, arguably the most long-standing and successful contract between a people and their government in history. When we follow it, it works. When we change it slowly, it positively impacts the most people. It is grounded in truth. Truth that no one can argue. God's word in our daily lives should be the same.

People should see us and ask, "How is it that you are so [fill in any fruit of the Spirit here: loving, joyful, peaceful, patient, kind, gentle and calm]?"

That is the time to share your testimony about how Jesus changed your life. If you are being interrogated or called names, simply ask why they feel that way. If they actually tell you, great! Be a panel moderator, not an activist with an agenda to destroy others. Most people who don't know God or hate Him have a painful story to share. When they finish, offer to pray for them. You'd be surprised how many will let you.

Jesus was the most inclusive leader of all time. People heard about His exploits and sought Him out. They changed because of His teaching and influence, not because He reprimanded them. A quick read of the Gospels and you will find that, deservingly so, He only chastised the Jewish leaders who wanted to kill Him. In spite of having positions to advocate for the Jewish people, the Pharisees sought to rip them off. Their hearts were only for their own interests. Those who were curious, like Nicodemus, Jesus educated.

Jesus taught truth. The truth. From the foundation of the world, His word continues to prevail over all the latest, clever teachings. Correctly deployed, God's truth will unify us, much like that which unifies any organization.

In business, the agreed upon doctrine is codified in mission, vision, and values.

How well do your business values align with your personal actions? How well do your daily habits align with your particular brand of faith? When faith, leadership—of yourself, your family, and your team—and business are under one doctrine of belief, your life becomes fully integrated. Body, mind, and Spirit are unified. God loves unity.

Synergy (the whole is greater than the sum of its parts) epitomizes what your life will look like as a faith-driven leader. In a fully integrated life, trust is the fruit. Wearing the same hat at home, work, and in the community synergizes your efforts. It is comparable to economies of scale in business.

> **Humans have a unique ability to master their mind, will, and emotions, regardless of what their five senses are telling them**

Changing your mindset and behaviors every time something around you shifts, merely reacting to external forces, makes you no different from any animal on planet earth. Humans have a unique ability to master their mind, will, and emotions regardless of what their five senses tell them.

My friend and former physical training coach, US Congressman John McGuire, was a Navy SEAL sniper instructor. As the founder of SEAL TEAM Physical Training, Inc., he taught us that the body always wants to conserve energy and resources. Thus, at only forty percent of capacity, it tells us that we are tired and need to rest and recharge.

Simply put, the physical senses lie! The five senses impact our emotions first, then our willpower, and finally our judgment. Ground up decision-making filters reduce the spirit to something man created.

Faith-driven leaders work from the top down. The US Constitution holds American citizens, who enjoy the freedoms of this country, to an obligation, a standard. Naturalized immigrants take the oath to support and defend it—just as elected officials and military personnel. It's what we rally around, what unifies us. Children are taught to pledge allegiance to the flag of the United States of America, and to the Republic for which it stands, one nation, under God, indivisible, with liberty and justice for all. The republic for which it stands, founded in the Constitution, is the highest authority in the US. It's the ideal.

Similarly, world-class business has to be grounded in truth. The operating procedures must align with a higher authority under which everyone unites.

Without the ideal, how else could we know when we've missed the mark? If a team member steals from petty cash or lies to a customer, how do we know that is wrong? If they live "their truth" and that involves breaking laws passed by the local legislature, can we fire them? If the truth about stealing is no longer held as a standard, then we won't be able to. If business leaders in America do not figure out how to hold elected officials, employees, and themselves to the highest standards of ethics and morals, even the idea of personal rights to safety are jeopardized.

Who loses most?

Women and children. Men do not attract attackers in most cases. Hyenas do not go after the strongest wildebeest. They go after the small, injured, or babies. This is an urgent matter. You cannot have a world-class business if your team members do not feel basic safety at work. Faith-driven leaders are the stopgap to this slippery slope. Doing the right thing should not be a gray area.

Ultimately, the responsibility for this madness is ours. Yes, us—Christian business leaders. Over the years, we funded the election campaigns for bad people.

I can hear it now, "I didn't elect them, Jerry!"

What did we do to intervene?

Nothing. For more than three decades, Christianity has seen an overall decline, but particularly in the workplace. Baby boomers and Gen X, our kids are the ones now in the workplace.

Why did we stop teaching our children?

It's not just parents. The universities, many of which were established on Christian doctrine, have long since abandoned their founding contracts. Their constitutions, the higher law to which they should defer, go unreferenced and unmentioned. They have been exporting countless leaders into the workplace without any moral footing. They are taught to define "good" and "bad" for themselves.

Defining "good" without submission to a higher authority, the lines get very blurred.

Is "good" what is good for me? Or for you?

How do we know we are good?

You might say, "Well, I think I'm good. I've never murdered anyone. I don't steal or lie, *mostly*." This is a common response.

When is it okay to lie, cheat, or steal?

When the former President of Harvard plagiarizes someone else's work and defends with "her truth," we can be sure that she believes she's a "good" person.

Fifty years ago, there was social capital in being a Christian in the workplace. Good or not, one was considered trustworthy if they were seen in the church pews or volunteering. Whatever brought someone into God's house of worship, I personally believe that they cannot remain unchanged by the visit. Thus, if someone's motives were evil, they sat through the sermon, served the meal, or donated money to look good in the face of others. That's more than nothing.

For me, however small, changes began. Motivated by greed, I accepted the Lord's call and became justified through faith. As I grow in the Lord, the process of sanctification strips away more and more of my original, evil intent. I went to Sunday service because I wanted wealth. Now I praise God through both high and low bank account levels! More on that later, but faith comes by hearing. You have to be physically present to hear anything.

Throughout the 1990s, we saw a shift toward indifference to one's faith in making decisions. Thus, attending church was no longer a necessary part of good business. As long as they were a "good" person and got the job done, it didn't matter. "Good" was well-established as those who do not lie, cheat, steal, and similar postulates. Those standards became *too* axiomatic.

Why?

Judeo-Christian values were so ingrained that America has forgotten where they came from.

How?

Schools and courtrooms stopped displaying the Ten Commandments. Parents and elected officials were unmoved or unaware of the link between business and faith. The Bible was no longer taught in universities. Subsequently, doing the right thing and the source of the law and its authority was lost. Over time, being a good person was reduced to whatever a flawed human being's feeling about good was in the moment.

Why didn't we speak up? Or speak louder?

Evangelists spoke very loud. They have for most of history. Why didn't we listen?

No one listens to a yell. TV and social media have been discredited as well.

How then, will we lead the world to Jesus?

You will probably never see me on a corner with a blow horn preaching the Gospel. Not that there is anything wrong with that calling. There's a percentage who are excited about that method of witness. If you can believe that every step of your life was preordained before the foundation of the world, then you are called, just like Jesus was, to evangelize and minister right where you are. Regardless of personality, skill sets, and desires, at work, home, and in the community, we need to be 100 percent Jesus' disciples. The people around you are there for a reason.

What about free will?

God has a perfect plan for your life, and the more of it you volunteer back to Him, the better it gets! In the coming chapters, you are going to learn more about why this is so important, what God says about business, and how to serve Him while remaining unified to your family, job, personality, upbringing, and beliefs.

From the top down, faith-driven leaders start with Jesus as CEO. Like any policymaker, His mission, vision, and values are what drives our decision-making, for ourselves, our families, our businesses, and communities. His mission—to go and make disciples—provides the vertical standard for our existence. His vision, that all people of every ethnicity be baptized in the name of the Father, Son, and filled with the Holy Spirit, provides the goal.

As my founding pastor, friend, and mentor Steve Stells likes to command us at the end of his classes, "Be bold, and do exploits in the name of Jesus!"

The Lord's value statements, the Ten Commandments, provide the blueprint for our activity and guide how we interact with Him and everyone else. God has a problem-solving process that guarantees growth in every area of life. He also cares deeply about money, metrics, and achieving goals. Further, I'll reveal multiple examples on how to operate in business as one person and simultaneously intersect faith, leadership, and business.

Parents out there know full well that your relationship with children grows richer as they mature. Parents who raise their kids to be people whom they want as best friends, make hard decisions about letting them learn through failure and discipline. God operates this way with His chosen. In case you any doubt, those reading *this* book are most certainly His chosen!

I like to say that leadership is an art and a science. It takes insight, intuition, organization, and planning. World class business, just as God does, addresses the qualitative and quantitative. From Genesis and the seven-day week to Revelation and 144,000, God is very precise and calculating. He also delegates and lets us fail. He knows that failure produces humility and humility produces wisdom. God wants a relationship with His family. As we grow in humility and wisdom, we grow more like Him.

> **Leadership is an art, requiring insight and intuition, also a science, which needs organization and planning**

To grow into the fullness of Christ at work, faith-driven leaders need to dive deep into faith and business and marry the two. From the most strategic to personal, daily decisions, we are obliged to discover how to implement those skills through others and truly multiply. Without firing a shot, holding a protest, or annoying a coworker, faith-driven leaders can leave both a kingdom legacy and one for the management of their business. In the next chapter, you will learn how this marriage between faith and business works and how you can apply it to your journey toward fulfilling your call as a faith-driven leader!

The Boardroom or Bible Study

For group discussion and individual journaling:

Have you ever felt like your business or job owned you? How did you react?

What does world class business look like to you?

How do you feel knowing that Jesus was an entrepreneur and a businessman before beginning his marketplace ministry? Why?

What jail-like, rock-bottom moment in your life turned around significantly because of God's grace and favor?

What is one situation when every bone in your body told you to run, but God told you to, "Be still and know that [He is] the Lord?"

When have you let sources other than God's word define truth? What was the result?

What steps do you take to master your mind, will, and emotions? What lies do your five senses consistently tell you?

How do you lead? As an art, with Insight and Intuition? Or as a science, with Organization or Planning? Which are most important? Why?

PART II

YOUR OBLIGATION TO EXECUTE: WHY FAITH-DRIVEN LEADERSHIP?

> The Lord our God has secrets known to no one. We are not accountable for them, but we and our children are accountable forever for all that he has revealed to us, so that we may obey all the terms of these instructions.
>
> -Deuteronomy 29:29

CHAPTER 5

A MARRIAGE OF FAITH AND BUSINESS

> "Success is stumbling from failure to failure
> with no loss of enthusiasm."
> –Winston S. Churchill

What does business have to do with faith? With God? Jesus? In Genesis, we read that God's first covenant with mankind was *before* the fall. God blessed them and directed mankind to "be fruitful, multiply and have dominion over the earth." This was, is, and will be His objective for us. Jesus, just before His ascension, gave a similar mission, "go and make disciples ..." (Gen. 1:28, Matt. 28:19).

God and His Son established the first covenant, gave us words, and ultimately taught us how to keep our word. Keeping our word and trusting that others will do the same is the foundation of business. So far, Jesus was the only person to completely keep His word. He agreed to remove his supernatural clothing, live with all the temptation of the flesh, overcome it, and allow himself to be murdered on a cross. Even harder was His descent into the belly of the beast to declare His reign over that realm as well (Phil. 2:6–7, Matt. 12:40, Col. 2:15).

Why would he do such a thing?

We've all read that He "so loved the world," and that is true (John 3:16). But He also gave His word. In Jesus' darkest hour, asking three times for the horrific cup to pass, He remained on mission, despite God's answer being no (Matt. 26:39–44). He didn't get angry at God and go commit a bunch of sinful acts.

As a human, how could He endure? How can we?

Faith. He was absolutely convinced of His father's good plan and promise of resurrection. Remember, Jesus had previously never died (that is, spiritually disconnected from His Father) and he had never been to hell. That's why he sweated drops of blood. He was far less concerned with the brutal assault than He was of being separated from His Father's spirit. Jesus' stress was due to the impending absorption of every sinful thought and action ever conceived or committed by mankind. All past, present and future evil coalesced in one moment as He was drained of His life-giving blood.

Solid evidence for this can be seen in the Apostle Paul's mission. He was whipped on five occasions, each with the same number of lashes, (forty minus one) and suffered worse physical punishment over a longer period of time than Jesus (2 Cor. 11:24). Paul's physical and mental punishment over his thirty year or so ministry was far worse than Jesus' twelve hours. Unlike Paul, Jesus "gave up His Spirit" (Matt. 27:50).

Remember when I said we might come to a screeching halt? This may be that moment for you. The reality is, Jesus was terrified of what lay ahead of Him. Fully man and fully God. Fully terrified and fully filled with the Holy Spirit.

As a Believer, have you ever been terrified?

I'm certain every one of us can recall moments of terror. Like Jesus before the cross and Paul, we are filled with the Holy Spirit. That is why Paul, the apostles, and every Christian will never suffer the way Jesus did. Even the prophets were in a holding pattern, so to speak. They could see and talk to those in hell, but not experience it (Luke 16:24–25).

Faith is the antidote to being paralyzed in fear. Like Jesus, we can walk right into certain death with confidence that God will deliver, sweating and with shaking knees, but pressing on! Those moments of dread and weakness, encountered without faith, are why we have so many absurd, ideological runaway trains, particularly in higher education and the marketplace. More on those will follow, but to protect everyone's right to life, liberty, and property, faith and business cannot be separated.

Faith provides the guidelines that make business work. Faith is grounded in God's word. His words have unlimited power. Similarly, and rooted in our faith, our words have a measure of power (Rom. 12:3).

Although many remain in poverty, and worse, we have seen an overall higher standard of living, an exponential birth rate improvement, and a more distributed level of opulence in the world. The last 2000 years have brought equal amounts of prosperity and horror. If we continue to pursue God and give Him the glory, then abundance in this life and the next will follow. Not without challenge, trial, and persecution, Jesus taught:

> Then Peter began to speak up. "We've given up everything to follow you," he said. "Yes," Jesus replied, "and I assure you that everyone who has given up house or brothers or sisters or mother or father or children or property, for my sake and for the Good News, will receive *now in return* a *hundred times* as many houses, brothers, sisters, mothers, children, and property—along with *persecution*. And in the world to come that person will have *eternal life*." (Mark 10:28-30, emphasis added)

Notice Jesus said, "now in return." Then he detailed the "hundred times" and added "persecution" and concluded with "eternal life." Following Jesus brings a massive multiplier to your life, both in grace and abundance, then persecution, and finally the ultimate prize of eternal existence with the Creator.

Let us not mistake, throughout history, omitting God for the sake of glory and wealth has brought great suffering. The last 100 years have seen more bloodshed than ever. Conversely, the worldwide standard of living has significantly improved, largely in part to the post WWII economic influence of the United States.

The United States was founded on God's word. What we call the Ten Commandments shaped the inspiration and motivation for the founding of the country. Our first president, George Washington, took an oath in God's name, repeatedly revered God in his inaugural address, and warned that if we departed from His word, we'd suffer. God's warning and inspiration to Joshua were the same:

> Be strong and very courageous. Be careful to obey all the instructions Moses gave you. Do not deviate from them, turning either to the right or to the left. Then you will be successful in everything you do. *Study* this Book of Instruction continually. *Meditate* on it day and night so you will be sure to *obey* everything written in it. Only then will you *prosper* and *succeed* in all you do. (Josh. 1:7-8, emphasis added)

From the scripture, we read five steps:

1. Study.
2. Meditate.
3. Obey.
4. Prosper.
5. Succeed.

Three of five steps to success require faith. Simply stated, you have to believe that what God says is true. Every business model ever invented requires the same process. Study your craft. Meditate or think about what it means for you. Obey or follow the plan. Then you will prosper or grow. Success is inevitable. Franchises have perfectly executed this for years.

World-class business requires faith-driven leaders. Faith-driven leaders submit to authority. I cannot overemphasize that those who are *under* authority, *have* authority. Their authority, their strength, fortitude, and their patience, come from God's word. Jesus' last declaration and command before his ascension encapsulate this well:

> **I cannot overemphasize that those who are under authority, have authority**

> Jesus came and told his disciples, "I have been given all *authority* in heaven and on earth. Therefore, go and make disciples of all the nations, baptizing them in the name of the Father and the Son and the Holy Spirit. Teach these new disciples to obey all the commands I have given you. And be sure of this: I am with you always, even to the end of the age." (Matt. 28:18-20, emphasis added)

Mission, vision, and values were all perfectly detailed before He left. And our authority is derived from His. Through Jesus, we are dispatched into the world to take back His territory from the enemy, Ha'Satan, His and our adversary.

World-class business requires faith-driven leaders who understand that it is not about them. It is not about their P&L statement. It is not about their goals. It is about the *Missio Dei* (mission of God), the Great Commission, and using His resources to carry that out.

I can hear it now, "We're Believers, Jerry, certainly not pastors. I have an MBA, and barely make it to church. How do I carry this out?"

Instead of constantly focusing on our P&L statement, let's read God's P&L statement. God provides Protection (P) and Leadership (L). David writes:

> The Lord is my shepherd; I shall not want.
> He makes me to lie down in green pastures;
> He leads me beside the still waters.
> He restores my soul;
> He leads me in the paths of righteousness
> For His name's sake.
> Yea, though I walk through the valley of the shadow of death,
> I will fear no evil;
> For You are with me;
> *Your rod and Your staff*, they comfort me.
> You prepare a table before me in the presence of my enemies;
> You anoint my head with oil;
> My cup runs over.
> Surely goodness and mercy shall follow me
> All the days of my life;
> And I will dwell in the house of the Lord
> Forever. (Ps. 23:1–6, NKJV)

The rod referenced here is our protection. A rod was a thick, short club the shepherd would swing or throw at would-be attackers, particularly wild animals, to prevent them from killing his flock. His staff was what he used to corral, guide, and even save lost sheep. World-class leaders rely on God and teach others to do the same.

Today, the government attempts to meet the needs of the community where the church once did. There was a time when pastors led the community and especially led the business owners. I imagine the church being the largest building in town. Pastors knew the business leader was in the world every day, behind enemy lines, immersed in all facets of bartering and financial transactions. Jesus detailed this battle 2000 years ago:

> No one can serve two masters. For you will hate one and love the other; you will be devoted to one and despise the other. You cannot serve God and be enslaved to money. (Matt. 6:24)

The battle ensues. Pastors lead the community with God's word to overcome their challenges. From natural disasters to temptations with money to raising a family, through God's word, they are called to keep our eyes on the eternal impact.

Like many of you, I am a business owner, executive leader, and member of a church. Those with our vocation have a unique perspective from which church leaders can benefit. Similarly, pastors have a role in the church not unlike ours in the marketplace.

Why aren't we learning and growing together?

In our agency, we have a program called *100X Church*. It means 100 percent healthy (or in the pursuit of) and X (meaning multiplication). Multiplication, not in the church planting sense, but multiplying healthy leaders into the marketplace, just as Jesus did. Peter and the other eleven all had occupations, and Paul made tents!

In *100X Church*, we hold marketplace leadership days, (½ day training seminars for everyone), quarterly or monthly at little to no cost to the church, other than perhaps refreshments. Anyone from the community is invited. Subsequently, church leaders and staff are organized into monthly or twice monthly growth groups with those from the congregation that have similar responsibilities in their jobs. Again, church staff participants do not pay any fees.

A consultant or coach leads the groups through our training curriculum that includes both secular leadership and biblical teachings. Church staff/leaders walk through the training with their marketplace counterparts from the community or congregation. Thus processing the same challenges and revelation, bridging the gap that has separated them from one another for so many years!

> **The church once again becomes the place someone learned to get promoted or improve their business**

The church now becomes that place where someone learned how to improve their business or get promoted. How much more cheerfully will they contribute to the bottom line then?

The marriage between faith and business is comparable to that between a husband and wife. Simply put, we make a commitment to go through a hard thing together—and see it through, not unlike raising children. We then help others do the same, at all walks of life, young and old, rich and poor.

Humans have always had the ultra-wealthy, and Jesus told Mary's critics over the alabaster jar, "we'll always have the poor" (Matt. 26:11). America's strength resides in its middle class. Lower to upper-middle class tend to be leaders in business, at all levels. With 61 million Americans working in the SMB, this is where the rubber meets the road for both evangelism and discipleship.

How will *100X Church* work if people have stopped coming to a Christian house of worship?

Many employees, leaders, and business owners who don't know God will never set foot in a building dedicated to worship of the Lord Jesus, often called church. Today, the new church is the marketplace. Surprisingly, the early church grew from the same.

Jesus was our first marketplace minister. On Faith and Finance, a Christian talk radio show from the Bott Radio Network, Rob West reports:

> It's probably not a coincidence that when Jesus called the 12 disciples, many of them owned and operated businesses as tradesmen and commercial fishermen. And consider where Jesus spent a lot of time during his earthly ministry. Of His 134 appearances, 122 of them are in the marketplace. He also told a total of 52 parables and 45 of them have a workplace context. And the practice of witnessing in the business world continued with the apostles. Of the 40 divine interventions recorded in the Book of Acts, 39 were in the marketplace.

The early church, or group of people following Jesus, was founded in merchant centers. In fact, the first 300 years of the church centered around what was called a "household" or "oikos" in Greek, not the ecclesia (Cockram, 2022). The assembly, as it was later known, developed long after the Romans made Christianity the national religion. The oikos (household), as a descriptor, was more of a merchant center. It included indentured servants, biological family members, neighbors, and other trade partners.

The early church also spread through what we call franchising today. When an indentured servant reached a point where they could be free, they could choose to be a bond servant and stay for life. Sometimes, the master would set them up in another area to continue the trade or mercantile operation. This underground network built the first system of believers who practiced *the way of Jesus* and became what we think of as house church.

This is where Phoebe, a benefactor, deaconess, and servant of the Lord Jesus in early Rome, would walk to and from, in the dark, villa to villa (Rom. 16:1-2). Scary stuff back then, particularly because everyone was an enemy of the early Christians. From the Jews to the Romans, and especially other business owners whose financial stability was based on the pagan religions of the time, Christ-bearers, or little Christs, were in constant peril.

The apostle Paul experienced great hardship and simultaneously brought tremendous glory to God. Luke describes a frequent scenario:

> One day as we were going down to the place of prayer, we met a slave girl who had a spirit that enabled her to tell the future. She earned a lot of money for her masters by telling fortunes. She followed Paul and the rest of us, shouting, "These men are servants of the Most High God, and they have come to tell you how to be saved." This went on day after day until Paul got so exasperated that he turned and said to the demon within her, "I command you in the name of Jesus Christ to come out of her." And instantly it left her. Her masters' hopes of wealth were now shattered, so they grabbed Paul and Silas and dragged them before the authorities at the marketplace. "The whole city is in an uproar because of these Jews!" they shouted to the city officials. "They are teaching customs that are illegal for us Romans to practice." (Acts 16:16-21)

Clearly, Paul acted impulsively, but he helped the slave girl. As you read, he completely destroyed her master's business model. They eventually went to prison and God enabled them to lead everyone to Jesus. God's glory was immense, but not without persecution.

Let's examine Lazarus, whose sisters were Mary and Martha. Martha was prepping for a meal and freaking out because Mary wasn't helping. There had to be enough people there to make her uncomfortable. If he were a well-known local merchant, equivalent to one of today's marketplace influencers, raising him from the dead would have gotten the most likes on social media. It was a miracle and a death sentence for the Lord, but it exemplifies why Jesus would hang out where lots of people gathered (Luke 10:40–42).

The inference is Lazarus was a business owner or entrepreneur. The *Chosen* TV series presents him as a building contractor who is friends with Jesus, the equivalent of a pastor. From the earliest days of Christianity, pastor and merchant lived, walked and fought together, side by side. The marketplace held a key role, strategically and at a personal level, in building the Body of Christ.

Friends of Jesus are those who "abide" or follow Him. Friends are who He died for. We can be His friend, but it comes with a cost. John details Jesus' explanation well:

> I have loved you even as the Father has loved me. Remain in my love. When you obey my commandments, you remain in my love, just as I obey my Father's commandments and remain in his love. I have told you these things so that you will be filled with my joy. Yes, your joy will overflow! This is my commandment: Love each other in the same way I have loved you. There is no greater love than to lay down one's life for one's friends. You are my friends if you do what I command. I no longer call you slaves, because a master doesn't confide in his slaves. Now you are my friends, since I have told you everything the Father told me. You didn't choose me. I chose you. I appointed you to go and produce lasting fruit, so that the Father will give you whatever you ask for, using my name. This is my command: Love each other. (John 15:9-17)

Jesus makes it simple. Love God. Love each other. With today's lack of faith and confusion over actual truth, referring back to God's original value statements is the best approach to living a Godly life in the marketplace.

The Big Ten, or Ten Commandments, combine faith and business perfectly. The first five deal with faith; what we call our *vertical* alignment. The second five are how we interact with others, or *horizontal* alignment. These two directions form a cross. Jesus dying on a cross was no coincidence. It symbolizes, among many other things, how to return to God's original design, with Jesus, His heart and yours, right in the center!

> **God's Big Ten combine faith and business perfectly, teaching us how to be leaders others want to emulate**

Put differently, the first five teach us how to be a leader others want to emulate. The second five govern the business world. This is how Jesus and a Hebrew teacher of the law discussed it:

> One of the teachers of religious law was standing there listening to the debate. He realized that Jesus had answered well, so he asked, "Of all the commandments, which is the most important?" Jesus replied, "The most important commandment is this: 'Listen, O Israel! The LORD our God is the one and only LORD. And you must love the LORD your God with all your heart, all your soul, all your mind, and all your strength.' The second is equally important: 'Love your neighbor as yourself.' No other commandment is greater than these." The teacher of religious law replied, "Well said, Teacher. You have spoken the truth by saying that there is only one God and no other. And I know it is important to love him with all my heart and all my understanding and all my strength, and to love my neighbor as myself. This is more important than to offer all of the burnt offerings and sacrifices required in the law." (Mark 12:28-33)

The Big Ten are merely an exposition of how to carry this out.

If you do not know God, it can be difficult to "love" Him. Today's overuse of the word love gives no clue either. With everyone defining their "own truth," there is no clear detail of how to love others. God revealed this solution 3500 years before we were born!

When we dig into the Big Ten and how to use them in business, it's noteworthy to look at Jesus' last phrase, "as yourself." This is the leadership component. You have to lead yourself appropriately if you are going to fulfill the Big Ten and "abide" in Jesus. The intersection of faith, leadership, and business comes directly from God's 10 *rules for life*. Long before the popular twelve of today, God had ten.

Every world-class business must first get this right. The 10 commandments, or 10 statements as the Hebrew translation indicates, are our ten rules for business as well. The first five get our faith and leadership in check and the last five are how we handle business, and others. We will call these, *The Big Ten for Business,* and they will launch us into the last half of the book. This is our how to guide for proper decision making.

We know what a faith-driven leader is, we know what a world-class business is, and we've touched on their relevance. Before we tackle the how, we must first expand on why and examine the runaway trains noted earlier. These issues deeply illustrate why faith-driven leadership is vital. Hotly contested topics were intentionally selected, as they are foundational to our faith, and it's no accident that they are considered controversial. Regardless of where you stand on each, as a Christ-bearer, keep an open mind!

The Boardroom or Bible Study

For group discussion and individual journaling:

Have you ever been in a situation like Joshua? If so, would God's guidance, Study, Meditate, Obey, Prosper, Succeed work for you? If not, would you step up? Why or why not?

When have you been compelled to speak up or speak out about injustice? Where did you get the authority to do so? How did you feel?

What do you or your church do to promote marketplace ministry? Why?

How do you feel about Old Testament law? Can it help you in daily life? Why or why not?

CHAPTER 6

WHY GOD'S BLUEPRINT: A FEW RUNAWAY TRAINS

> "A true leader has the confidence to stand alone,
> and the courage to make tough decisions."
> -Douglas MacArthur

The American marketplace has been infected with a disease as insidious as cancer. Relativism is eating our faith alive. Relativism is the belief that there are no absolute truths. First deployed in academia, then in business and public education, its contamination culminated with the church and the family unit. The disengagement of our culture from truth through the latter half of the 20th century, and into this one, has birthed multiple runaway trains with which to contend. It is not the scope of this book to cover them all, but examining a few of the most controversial, we find they slid off the rails due to one primary issue. There is no standard.

Something deep inside us knows that standards are important. We can feel it, but with the ease in not holding a standard, and with society's permission, we capitulate. Today, there are individuals graduating from seminary that have not accepted Jesus as Lord, nor have participated in a public water baptism. They conclude as well that Jesus is but one of many paths to God. These three functions are the foundation for acceptance of our faith.

Those who are not Christ followers may conclude the same. But to be a follower of the way of Jesus, is by definition an acceptance of His teachings, foundational of which is that He is the One truth, life, and way (John 14:6).

I will note that the thief on the cross was not baptized and still joined Him in paradise, but different than him, teachers are held to a higher standard. Or were.

Why should I accept Jesus if He's not Lord? Why follow His ways at all?

These are logical and important questions if we do not adhere to the basic standard. The answer is you shouldn't.

If someone claims Christianity and simultaneously does not claim Him as Lord, particularly if they are in a Christian leadership position, then it is not Christianity. It is by definition relativism, and they made up their own version. That is called a cult. It is not the focus of this book, but Jesus' life, death, and resurrection are all historical facts. Those claims are proven beyond the standards of any other facts we hold as true events. Our faith is based on facts. Unfortunately, when standards based on fact are no longer revered, confusion becomes the norm. That is the first train flying off the rails.

The desperation to win, to reach one's own personal goal, has led people to devise cunning methods of cheating for the sake of perceived victory. These days, men pretend to be women, just so they can compete in women's sports, hoping they can claim superiority. Men are physically stronger than women.

Are those men really winning?

Unequivocally, no. If you are a female athlete who worked her entire life, pursuing an obvious calling and capitalizing on God-given talent, I salute you. In no rational universe should you have that ripped away because some weak-minded official didn't want to face the potential conflict of not affirming someone's choice of gender that day.

Why blame the official and not the pretending athlete?

We've had people with gender dysphoria long before it was a problem in women's sports. It wasn't until someone was bullied into false affirmation that it caused an issue.

> **We've had people with gender dysphoria long before it was an issue in women's sports, but we allowed ourselves to be bullied into false affirmation**

For the rest of us, how would you feel?

I'm a parent of four highly athletic and competitive children, two of whom are daughters. I have watched them work tirelessly to reach their full potential. If it were them, I would be outraged. I am outraged.

Luckily for my oldest daughter, who was a competitive gymnast for ten years, it takes too long to develop high level female gymnastics skills to warrant a male's invasion. She recently said, "All he'd have to do is split the bar once." The implication is obvious.

Equally fortunate for my oldest son, football is resistant for obvious reasons. Please understand, I have no issue with members of the opposite sex participating as appropriate. To do so on false pretenses, while everyone around them is expected to go along with the charade, is how the train leaves the tracks.

When the pursuit of one's goals are permitted to override truth, humans will go to any length to consider themselves winners. Without high moral and ethical standards, we have proven that ego, and the reliance on self, will justify the most nonsensical claims. Taken to the extreme, standards that are rooted in biology are now being called social constructs. Another train derailed.

Let's briefly look at the science.

Since the Age of Enlightenment beginning in the 1700s, with the use of the scientific method, science has brought considerable discovery to humanity. It is worth noting that the Age of Enlightenment's greatest contributors were Christian. Yet today, long-held truths about men and women are being overlooked. Sports are largely based on competition requiring intense physical training and improvement. However, the rationale for men competing in women's sports is based on a non-evidence based, philosophical perspective, not physical or even psychological characteristics. Thus, science is being reimagined (now my least-favorite verb), or completely ignored in the pursuit of a personal or group agenda, not worthy ideals.

In a comment from the *American Psychologist*, a peer reviewed journal, researchers Michelle A. Cretella of the American College of Pediatricians, and her colleagues, have written:

> In addition to sex-specific genes found on the sex chromosomes, scientists have identified at least 6,500 shared genes that are expressed differently throughout the body depending on whether the subject is male or female. [Note the binary reference] This sex differential gene expression has been identified in at least 53 different tissues, including brain tissue (Gershoni & Pietrokovski, 2017). In other words, macroscopic similarities between male and female body systems notwithstanding, organ tissues are sexually dimorphic

at the molecular/hard-drive level due to sex specific genes and sex differentially expressed genes that are present at fertilization (Gershoni & Pietrokovski, 2017). In fact, brain gene transcription has been found to be sexually dimorphic across the life span, and the biggest male–female difference for many genes occurs during the prenatal period. (Kang et al., 2011)

Friends, that is a very academic way of confirming God's revelation in Genesis that we are male and female—from the moment of fertilization. Every molecule in the body is built, from conception, around that starting point.

Proponents of a non-binary gender perspective will argue that gender is different from biological sex. First, the word gender, as it relates to biology, was adopted in the 20th century merely to replace the descriptive phrase biological sex. During that time, the word sex came to reference those activities in eroticism (Etymology Dictionary: gender). It was not used for psychological purposes. However, all elements that physiologically impact psychology are also rooted in prenatal, binary attributes at the biochemical, cellular level. The Institute of Medicine writes:

Basic genetic and physiological differences, in combination with environmental factors, result in behavioral and cognitive differences between males and females... Studies relying on biological materials would benefit from a determination and disclosure of the sex of origin of the material, and clinical researchers should attempt to identify the endocrine status of research subjects. Longitudinal studies should be designed to allow analysis of data by sex. Once studies are conducted, data regarding sex differences, or the lack thereof, should be readily available in the scientific literature. Interdisciplinary efforts are needed to conduct research on sex differences. (2001)

To summarize, biological sex matters in every area of research. These citations were intentionally chosen because they are not specifically addressing the controversy. There is no bias from the authors. They merely point out the origins of every cell, the biochemical component of humanity and the scientific and medical importance of a binary approach to research, with regard to every tissue in the body, regardless of size or function.

Spiritually, we know where God stands on two genders. Behaviorally, cognitively, and psychologically, we have now read what scientists conclude about the importance of retaining two genders. Biochemically, and physically, two genders remain. Conclusively, because every cell in the human body is developed, from conception, around either the XX or XY chromosome, you cannot be born in the wrong body.

Karl Jung, Kathrine Briggs, and Isabel Myers produced research that revealed what they called "thinkers and feelers." Simply put, seventy percent of women tend to make decisions based on people and values, whereas seventy percent of men tend to make decisions based on systems and logic. However, there are men who have a presupposition toward feelings and women who are thinkers. This does not conclude they were born in the wrong body.

Regardless, if one attempts to redefine gender beyond its original dichotomy, as the research is continually re-proving to be incorrectly assigned, everyone is born one or the other. There are only two. To separate gender from biological sex is merely a redefining of words. No amount of physiological or environmental implementation is going to change each cell in one's body. Thus, it matters in research and is a significant component of psychology.

Gender dysphoria and same-sex attraction remain scientific representations of an abnormality consistent with any other present in this fallen world. For example, alcoholism is now called Alcohol

Use Disorder, but the symptoms, treatment, and impact on the lives it damages remain the same. Neither are based on some oppressive societal construct.

To abandon the foundational male-female dichotomy ultimately leads the next generation to tremendous confusion. Jordan Peterson, renowned psychologist and author, has consistently remarked that to be male or female is more foundational to life than even being a human. To convince someone that fact is not true is synonymous to convincing them of anything. In matters of interpreting Christian faith and Torah, I do not always agree with Dr. Peterson. In psychology, however, he has more than established himself as both learned and credible.

On the contrary, if an adult man or woman, age twenty-five or older, decides to dress differently than the norm, they get no judgment from me. It is the same as choosing a unique hairstyle. Regarding restroom use, let the body parts dictate. If you can stand without voiding on your leg, then pursue the urinal.

> **To abandon the male-female dichotomy ultimately leads the next generation to tremendous confusion**

Homosexual behavior between two consenting adults does not warrant my judgment, either. That is God's department. I do not condone it, nor practice it, but I believe all of us have fleshly desires that need to be brought captive under the obedience of Christ. As Believers, we are called to love God, love others, and let the Holy Spirit convict new Christians to a lifestyle change. Not one of us is righteous before Christ. No, not one.

I'd like to offer one quick note about God's judgment. After the resurrection and ascension of Jesus, and before His return, God's wrath is not exhibited in fire and brimstone or any of the

Old Testament manifestations. Contrary to what many alarmists would like to say, today's calamity and disasters are not overt divine judgment. His wrath is merely allowing you to pursue your desire. And there are consequences. When you use your body parts differently than intended, they get prematurely damaged. The consequence of bad decision-making is the wrath (Rom. 1:21–28).

Speaking of damage, my personal issue is with those who insist on confusing children. Where my righteous indignation, judgment, and opinion begin is with predatory behavior. As a researcher and healthcare practitioner, I am bound by multiple standards of ethics in research, mitigating harm, and mandatory reporting requirements. The red flags present today are widespread.

When children are influenced to "try on" another gender, they are convinced to engage in chemical or surgical treatment that cannot be reversed. They are damaged, not healed. The independent review boards who allowed this research to pursue deserve whatever consequence manifests upon them.

Cognitively, adolescent executive decision-making skills are largely undeveloped until early adulthood. Janet Warren in the *APA Handbook of Psychology and Juvenile Justice* writes:

> In contrast, reasoning—the 'cognitive capacities to process information' (Grisso, 2000, p. 157)—and judgment—the 'processes of attaching differential importance to various possible consequences of decisions' (Grisso, 2000, p. 159)—are two integrative functions that are developmentally and age specific. These two functions are central to legal decisional capacity and are pivotal in understanding why adolescents do not reach the same decisions as adults (Bonnie & Scott, 2013; Cauffman & Steinberg, 2012; Grisso, 2000). Furthermore, they help to explain why other aspects of psychosocial development, such as emotion regulation (Mayzer, Bradley, Rusinko, & Ertelt, 2009),

can tax the decision-making abilities of children and adolescents, particularly when they are faced with high-stress and complex situations. (Redlich, 2007; Warren, et al., 2016)

The decision to change one's gender is typically brought on by high stress, and it is certainly a complex situation.

Christopher F. Rufo, a senior fellow at the Manhattan Institute, contributing editor of City Journal, and a distinguished fellow of Hillsdale College, reports in their publication *Imprimis*, that clinical experimenters, as far back as the early 1980s in Chicago, targeted low income, single parent children. In many cases, the legal guardian lacked education and suffered themselves from drug or alcohol addiction, or mental challenges. Thus, the adults tasked with the care of children often possessed limited cognitive abilities. With regard to the doctors and researchers pushing the treatment, their cognitive abilities, however warped by pride, were fully developed.

Hippocratic oath, anyone?

Speaking of which, you can discover a multitude of facts and statistics about this runaway train at www.donoharmmedicine.org.

Nevertheless, parents who have grown children will attest to the insanity of teenagers, but will agree that behavior is virtually eliminated by age twenty-five. Not only that, but to "try on" another gender before they have matured to the one in which they were born, is an egregious error. There are countless cases of gender dysphoria where symptoms subside following puberty.

Leave the kids alone, let them decide, but only when they are fully grown and able. God ordained free will for adults. Beyond early adulthood, perhaps age twenty-five, if you still choose the path, who am I to object?

Where else is confusion rampant?

In the American marketplace, particularly institutions of higher learning, fear has replaced faith. Decisions based on ethnicity and gender replace those previously based on the content of our character. Speech codes are commonplace. To appease the tide of wokeness, administrators, business owners, and executives are operating out of alarm instead of conviction. Despite the highly controversial nature of most DEI&A training doctrine, public institutions have coerced individuals and organizations to adopt programs and curriculum that have not been officially validated, or worse, have condoned doctrine that contains critical race theory (CRT) and other nonfactual claims.

Why were the majority of reputable institutions so quick to adopt unreviewed policy which completely contradicted the 14th Amendment and the Civil Rights Act of 1964?

Fear.

Fearful leaders have adopted training that does more harm than good. Moreover, racial tensions have increased, further evidence of the error. There is a place for inclusivity training, but not at the expense of one group over another.

CRT and many DEI programs completely undermine the work of the Lord Jesus and that of Dr. Martin Luther King, Jr. What's more, those teaching quality cultural awareness have been completely obliterated by the tsunami of bad actors in the industry. The oft-quoted Dr. King himself said, the goal of true education is both intelligence and character. We have witnessed a lack of both. As a result, the absence of standard has released yet another runaway train, eroding good judgment within the American populace.

> **The absence of a standard has eroded good judgment in the American populace**

In addition to poor outcomes, lacking fact-based intelligence and respect for others, this movement has wasted countless resources.

Those resources could have been devoted to community and capital improvements, employee raises and bonuses, and charity. In an effort to avoid tough conversations aimed toward unifying those with differing ethnicity, countless dollars are being spent on divisive training. Eric Hammer from the Virginia Association of Scholars reports:

> At the two universities [In Virginia] where 2021 information was publicly available, the single year-over-year increase in DEI spending from 2020 to 2021 surged by at least 82%. James Madison University: 33 administrators at $2,566,326 in 2020 to 65 administrators at $5,302,266 in 2021. University of Virginia: 38 administrators at $4,149,732 in 2020 to 77 administrators at $6,924,279 in 2021. Estimates greatly understate the costs: These estimates are based on salary, not the full dollar costs to the employer, and are thus exclusive of benefits, payroll taxes, and so on. They also exclude other costs for activities, including overhead and countless hidden and miscellaneous expenditures to implement DEI ideology such as required training (including for orientation), mandatory programs for employees, on-campus councils, on-campus centers, and unidentified DEI administrators.

As if 33 administrators wasn't enough, 65? And 38 to 77? JMU and UVA are state-funded schools. Therefore, taxpayers are bearing the burden of an unconstitutional expense from which no one benefits. Even those employed in this field ultimately lose. He goes on to note the decrease in productivity from faculty and staff is immeasurable. According to the Washington Examiner, federal expenditures on DEI training in 2023 exceeded $16 million.

How did we get here?

Dread. Confusion. Lack of standard. Lack of courage. Lack of faith. As we've learned in the last decade, these are slippery slopes that lead to irreversible damage.

It's bigger than just those issues. I'm not marginalizing the sanctity of women's sports, workplace privacy, or equal opportunity. My goal is to elevate those concerns and institute a standard based on absolute truth.

Why?

The attack on hard work and meritocracy is causing an imminent national security threat. The attack on the family unit will destroy the future of humanity.

Do I really need to point out that the number one way to preserve the future growth and safety of any community is a loving family that teaches children right from wrong?

Apparently today, it is not so obvious. Christians who do not know Jesus, boys told they are girls, child mutilation, demonization of individuals based on skin color, and taxpayer money spent on divisive training are all runaway trains that destroy the lives of everyone.

How do we build a future of inclusivity when women are being excluded from their own sports? How do we build a future generation when men and women do not understand the biological differences associated with their gender? How do we build a future at all when everyone is divided into tiny subgroups based on external characteristics that have no bearing on personal interests, Godly calling, or potential?

> **To not win, in the Judeo-Christian faith, is to cease to exist**

Despite the tone and urgency, I am assuredly not opposed to training that teaches us to understand different cultures before judging them! Moderating a DEI&A symposium panel detailed exactly how much I'm willing to listen, participate, and lead through the most controversial of dialogue. Furthermore, I learned it directly from Jesus and God's word.

Despite what lies we feed ourselves to make the mirror easier to bear, you know it, I know it, God knows it; winning is everything. Yes, *winning is everything*. We must conquer the spirit of fear and confusion within ourselves. To not win, in the Judeo-Christian faith, is to cease to exist.

Sound too extreme?

You may not believe it, but we are all in a fight for our lives. Losing means a life of fear, bondage, and ultimately slavery, maybe not tomorrow or next year, but certainly in the next twenty.

Where will this country be then?

Take the case of Israel. No nation, culture, or people group on earth has been more persecuted for longer. Yet, they not only survive, but thrive. In *Why the Jews*, Dennis Prager explains what has infuriated their enemies for millennia is the basic claim they are God's chosen people. In an interview with Hugh Hewitt, Haviv Rettig Gur of the *Times of Israel* states that Jews enrage the world because they are the minority that succeeds. Israel proves that being small and outnumbered doesn't give you an excuse to lose (2023; 2024).

Although not always celebrated by those claiming the Christian faith, many of us agree and believe that Israel is God's chosen, with the corollary that they carried the seed, bloodline, and word that manifested the Messiah, Jesus of Nazareth, as God's Son. And His followers get to join that family. (Deut. 7:6, Rom. 11:17–24)

Regardless of the persecution or what circumstances they have to overcome, not unlike Americans, in times of difficulty, they operate in cultural unity. They are unified around their God and culture, a fact which is inconvenient at best and jeopardizes their very existence! Internally, and not unlike many democratic societies, America included, their government is in seemingly perpetual chaos.

Defending their right to exist and their cultural values—no one has done it longer. They take a beating, then they get tough. Marines, and any other benevolent warrior minded group, can respect that.

I'll note that I've never served overseas and did not deploy to combat. I was stationed at a training command in 29 Palms, CA. Therefore, my comment here is second hand, but from what I'm told, Israeli Defense Force (IDF) personnel carry immense respect amongst the US armed services. Former Israeli Prime Minister, Naftali Bennett in a podcast conversation with Jordan Peterson agrees. Paraphrasing he said, "In a lot of areas, public education being one of them, Israel is mediocre at best. Not with the IDF, that is where we shine" (2024).

They are devoted, well-trained and brilliant. Just when you think they've capitulated, they execute some strategic blow you never thought of! In an effort to maintain peace for as long as possible, they are often mistaken as weak. The specific instance will be covered later, but Abraham, the father of our faith, also executed night operations and had his own special forces, 318 of them to be exact!

My friend and fellow author, David L. Robbins, specializes in historical fiction novels. He has founded multiple non-profits, one of which is called *The Mighty Pen Project*. It's a free collegiate-level creative writing class for veterans, hosted by the Virginia War Memorial. In one of our many conversations over the years, he stated, "Historically we Jews had everything stolen from us and couldn't even own property. The only thing that couldn't be taken was our intellect. So we have, for thousands of years, excelled at things that require strong minds" (2020).

Furthermore, Jews follow a set of standards that God laid out for them over three millennia ago. In Genesis to Deuteronomy, also known as Torah, we read that as long as Jews adhered to His standards and put God first, they won. Still today, for them, winning is everything. It has to be. Surrounded by mortal enemies who perpetually plot their complete annihilation, if they lose, they cease to exist. Because of these constraints, despite their size, they are well-trained, prosperous, and consistently remain leaders in business, agriculture, and technology.

Unlike Israel, America had forgotten its standards. Separated from the world by two large oceans and the end of the Cold War, we thought we were immune to assault. The terrorist attacks on September 11, 2001, changed that perspective, but horror fades with each generation. Despite the severity of that tragedy, we still do not operate in a state of readiness. Israel is in a perpetual state of armed awareness.

It's no surprise the IDF, from God's chosen, cleverly attacked their enemy, only killing or injuring combatants, with no civilian casualties, by exploding their pagers and walkie-talkies. How creative! I do not encourage killing and maiming, but defending one's right to exist against those who have killed countless Jewish innocents and pledged eradication of the Jewish people and nation—they need to be stopped. Not only that, and what the public forgets is that Hezbollah, Israel's target, had been launching missiles at them for nearly a year before they retaliated.

Like 9/11 in the US, 10-7 or October 7th, 2023, in Israel, was a horrific attack against a peaceful population. Poor US foreign policy with Iran, the Middle East's principal exporter of terrorism, allowed China to buy oil from them and indirectly funded Hezbollah and the Hamas terrorists. Women were raped, babies were slaughtered, resulting in over 1200 Israeli deaths, and hundreds of hostages, some American citizens. All unprovoked.

Make no mistake, there is good and evil in the world. There is a standard, an absolute truth. Terrorist states that oppress their people, train, and fund murder operations, should not be traded with. Terrorists should not be trained and funded. Babies' heads should not be cut off. Women should not be raped.

Evil combatants who only use strength and force, not diplomacy, only respond to strength and force. Yet somehow, there are pro-Hamas and anti-Semitic protests shutting down American college campuses. It is not free-speech when you are preventing students from pursuing the education for which they worked so hard. Speak your mind, even if it angers another, but let them go to class. More will be covered later on how faith-driven leaders could have prevented the rise of this particular evil in the first place.

Presently, how is this possible?

From a spiritual and pragmatic perspective, we have forgotten the truth. A battle rages daily. Like Israel, followers of Christ are surrounded. We think the only dangers are existential. The threats are internal. Starting with the why behind our daily habits, we are surrounded by negative influences. These influences encourage us to pursue power over others, wealth for ourselves, and hedonism like never before.

Jerry, how do my daily decisions result in Hamas killing babies?

It starts small. Here are some questions I had to personally contend with but are a great microcosm for every believer's lifestyle choices. By the way, this was well into my walk with the Lord.

Why did I watch every season of Game of Thrones, more than once? Was that God honoring? It's harmless, right? How late was I up binge-watching? How productive was I the next day? Where does it end?

Here's the facts: I inundated myself with explicit scenes of sex, violence, gore, treachery, and pure evil. I stayed up too late and was tired, with less willpower and self-control. As a result, and as a married man, did my glance at someone of the opposite sex linger just a little too long the following day?

Perhaps.

Maybe it was harmless, but if I repeat this process tomorrow, will it get worse? Will I have less self-control when it comes to decisions that truly matter?

There is no evidence to suggest that my willpower against abuse and self-aggrandizement will improve without intentionality. Any person who thinks otherwise is fooling themselves.

What about our elected officials that have succumbed to their lust for more power?

It starts small. Tiny, seemingly insignificant behaviors have an exponential impact over time. Although temptations seem external, the choice is always internal, and the catalyst is spiritual. Our unseen mortal enemy loves to grease the path to our destruction, and he's everywhere.

Conversely, if Jesus proved anything, it's that one person can make a difference. Not just Him, but each of His disciples changed countless lives. Their disciples after have multiplied that impact.

> **Our unseen mortal enemy loves to grease the path to our destruction, and he's everywhere**

For them and us, it begins with daily decision-making. Victory in your daily decision-making is ground zero.

Winning this battle reveals truth, provides wisdom, and increases grace. Every day, we must be on full alert to counter the slippery slope of relativism, in our personal lives and the workplace. There is an antidote and a procedure to follow. This book is your field guide to executing both practical and inspirational processes for winning. Ultimately, we will stop the runaway train in our families, businesses, and communities. We will change the world.

Changing the world may not be a goal of yours, but existentially, we are closer to losing the good fight than ever before. Worldwide, freedom of speech is nearly lost. Our first, most inalienable right, the one God modeled for us "In the beginning ..." by speaking His word into existence, is under constant attack.

The digital landscape further represents the most obvious battleground. Domestically, there are many who celebrate banning "hate speech" and eliminating "misinformation." This is code for 'a higher governing authority will decide for us what is hate speech and what is misinformation.'

Ironically, John Kerry, whose illustrious political career included being former Lieutenant Governor of Massachusetts, United States Senator, United States Secretary of State, and the 2004 Democratic presidential nominee, built a life on being able to express himself as he deemed appropriate. At the World Economic Forum, he complained that the first amendment was a "major block" to hammering out misinformation. In 2021, Alexandria Ocasio Cortez (AOC) stated in an Instagram live video, "We're going to have to figure out how to reign in the media," to prevent, "misinformation and disinformation," from being spewed out.

What? How can common ground be found if an opposing argument is unheard? How do we know something is "hate speech," "fake news," and "misinformation," if we don't hear it? Who decides?

Outrageous? Hopefully, it's terrifying. Examples of this, the most dangerous of runaway trains, are everywhere.

Scary as it may be, we can switch tracks and course-correct in one generation. Jesus' example of fierce loyalty to God and bleeding passion for his friends and all humans provides the antidote. If we follow God, and put others first, the next generation will follow suit.

How to lead like Jesus is the primary focus of this book, but let's take one more chapter to examine the runaway trains' contemporary origins and wrap up "why" faith-driven leadership has such personal, yet concurrent global, significance.

The Boardroom or Bible Study

For group discussion and individual journaling:

When have you been emotionally bullied into compromising your values? How did you manage it?

Do you think the exclusive male/female dichotomy is important? Why or why not?

In your sphere of influence, where has the erosion of standards impacted you most? How are you walking through that valley with God?

What does winning look like to God? Is winning the most important thing to God? Why or why not?

What are three instances recently where you've seen the enemy greasing the path to your destruction? How did you overcome? If you did not, what will you do differently next time?

CHAPTER 7

FAITH'S GEOPOLITICAL IMPORTANCE

"The most fundamental problem of politics is not the control of wickedness but the limitation of righteousness."
–Henry Kissinger

In the years following World War II, America enjoyed prosperity driven by two major circumstances. The returning veterans and their families were simply fed up with scarcity and of wartime sacrifices. Thus, demand for consumer products skyrocketed and jobs were plentiful. Fortunately, America did not experience war on its soil. Other than Pearl Harbor and the terrorist attacks on September 11, 2001, it has not for over a hundred years. But the rest of the world still needed things.

Most of the developed nations were devastated and had great need for manufactured goods. This worldwide demand encouraged an abundance of US exportation. These circumstances spiked the growth of the middle class. Families had surplus. Veterans also took advantage of the G.I. Bill to further their education, thereby increasing the intellectual capital of America.

Unfortunately, intellect is where we got off track. As far back as President Woodrow Wilson, in an effort to engineer a perfect society, progressive politicians had increasingly implemented systems that gave governing authority to unelected experts. The emphasis shifted to consider the letter of the law rather than the spirit of the law. As a result, the proverbial letter count exponentiated. As government grew, so did regulation.

The more specialized an expert, the less they truly know about general governance, particularly at the local level. An intellectual living in the bubbles around the five American cities previously noted, Boston, New York, San Francisco, Los Angeles, and Washington, DC, cannot govern the lives of those with whom they have no contact (Murray, 2012).

Keeping power for governance at the lowest level allows people to regulate their lives in a way that is best for them. Freedom in governance impacts daily life with the same synergy that freedom in business impacts economic growth.

> **Freedom in governance impacts daily life with the same synergy that freedom in business impacts economic growth**

Locally elected officials, who pass laws with which their constituents agree, have a wide and broad knowledge base (the people living in their communities) from which to draw their decision-making. Nationally, laws need to stay simple. Sustainable and applicable rules can cover a wide range of demographics and geographies.

Larry Arnn, historian, professor and president of Hillsdale College, in an interview with Hugh Hewitt on *Hillsdale Dialogues*,

October 11, 2024, perfectly pinpoints the issue as one instigated with the election of Franklin Delano Roosevelt (FDR) and his "New Deal." He said:

> Our current government became the majority in the election of 1932. In 1930, the government was 12% of the economy, federal, state and local. Today it's over 50%. Back then, 60% of the money that was raised was raised and spent in the cities, counties and towns, which means there wasn't that much government. The government that was in existence was closest to the people. Today, it's less than 20% [raised and spent locally]. The federal government was less than 25% [of that] in 1930, now it's more than 60%. That's an increase of two-thirds.

Known as the administrative state, it's out of control. The most obvious evidence is the national deficit. Interest alone, now nearing a trillion dollars, will soon reign as the largest portion of the budget.

It took decades, but these experts wielded growing power over the daily lives of Americans. When a new US President is elected, about 3,000 transitions in federal personnel come with them. I always encourage people to vote for the platform, not the candidate. Personal emotions surrounding candidates can cloud the importance of issues on which the 3,000 will be working. Voting for the platform ensures that you get the 3,000 you want to decide what the next four years entail. Outside of that, the Office of Personnel Management (OPM) governs the pool of decision makers in a federal population of over 2.8 million employees.

OPM has a complex hierarchy and hiring process. It is beyond the scope of this book to detail that structure. Let's summarize by saying, its initial design was to shield agency leaders from political influence.

That is a good thing, right? Yes and no.

Flipped upside down, decision makers instituted as agency leaders technically work for that agency. However, they are not often chosen by the elected officials or the appointees tasked to lead those agencies. Thus, they are endowed with authority to govern the lives of everyday citizens without direct congressional oversight and unending federal tenure.

Through taxes and bureaucracy, administrative control exponentiated. For multiple decades, armed federal officers, from non-elected government agencies, such as the Department of Commerce, Department of Agriculture, and the Department of Energy, have been disturbing the lives of Americans. More details on the extent of this can be found in the book, *Over Ruled: The Human Toll of Too Much Law*, co-written with the legal scholar Janie Nitze and now Justice Gorsuch. An additional resource is *American Leviathan* by Ned Ryun.

These agencies and offices were capable of subverting due process for its citizens by interpreting the laws within themselves and executing on their decisions independent of judicial interpretive oversight. Recent effects of this were seen in the Covid crisis; imposing mask mandates and determining whether or not a business is considered essential.

As a business owner multiple times over, I can tell you that all of my businesses are essential—even if only to my family, employees, and customers. Thankfully, the US Supreme Court has begun to curtail this practice, by ending what was known as Chevron deference. The court cases detailing the initiation of this practice and its end are, respectively: 1984-Chevron U.S.A., Inc. v. Natural Resources Defense Council, Inc., and Loper Bright Enterprises v. Raimondo, decided on June 28, 2024.

But why is intellect a bad thing?

Intelligence to improve the lives of ourselves and others is not at all bad. From the manipulation of fire, the invention of the wheel, to air conditioning and clean water, human life on this planet has thrived as a result of innovation. When intellect and experts alone become that which predetermines the choices of everyday humans, ultimately, we all suffer.

This is why free speech is so critical. To bring a grievance before an elected ruling person or body is consistent with God's original design for the Jews leaving Egypt. The tribe leaders were chosen by their people and were considered fair and just. First in Exodus, then in Deuteronomy, we see an emphasis on rulers that were considered representatives of a group and subject to their demands, yet still under the Law, the supreme standard from God.

> **When the leader of a people is subordinated under God and the people, they uphold the ideal and deploy the will of the people**

When the leader of a people is subordinated to an authority greater than themselves and the will of the people, he or she makes decisions that uphold the ideal and deploy the will of the governed. However, the people and the elected leader must seek that higher model together. In the case of the Jews, it was God's law. It is that which is considered good—as defined by an absolute truth—and promotes general welfare.

Dr. Arnn notes in another *Hillsdale Dialogues* episode with Hugh Hewitt, that the 20th century, and the rise of experts who attempt to engineer society, has brought more death and destruction than all of that in known human history. He postulates that deference to experts for governance and the reliance on socialist ideology accounted for the death of not only six million Jews, but 30 million Russians under Lenin and Stalin, and upwards of 60 million Chinese under Mao Zedong. These leaders, and their electorate, did not seek the higher good.

The *Wall Street Journal*, in an article from Nov. 6, 2017, estimates that the Bolshevik plague to Petrograd, that is, the German Kaiser's exportation of Lenin and his party affiliates to St. Petersburg in 1917, led to the deaths of 100 million due to communism's grip on the eastern world in subsequent years.

How did these experts, who were runaway trains in their own right, maintain control? They made it illegal to share ideas. Those ideas considered "dangerous" to people were, in fact, more dangerous to the governing authority.

Following the 1960s, as the world got back on its feet and demand for American-made products waned, government intervention to *manufacture* a better society increased. Communism took root all over the world, and its ideologies infiltrated American academia at the highest levels. As those students left the university, the expert driven ideologies entered the workplace and government offices, particularly within the fringes of politics.

As we progressed into contemporary political regimes, and Leninist communism failed worldwide, experts still reigned supreme in most progressive organizations. The belief in the oft-cited "invisible hand principle" of Adam Smith's *Wealth of Nations* was replaced with two frameworks. Historically, on the right, large corporations only saw the working person as a number to improve the bottom line. Historically left leaning, labor unions perceived that the common working man needs an intermediary to take care of him. Neither embraced the desires, opinions, and decision-making capacity of the people themselves, most notably, the middle class. Only the experts truly knew what was best.

In more recent history, Dr. Jay Bhattacharya, in an interview with the Hoover Institute titled *On the Fight Against COVID Lockdowns*, estimates that over 100 million starvations occurred during the Covid economic shutdowns.

How?

It wasn't those of us in modern countries with Door Dash and laptops, it was those in third world, underdeveloped countries. Suddenly, they had no access to jobs in factories, refineries, or local goods and services that provided their wages. Travel destinations experienced catastrophic tourism losses.

What was the foundational cause of this poor decision-making?

Experts. When people are not allowed to make decisions based on what they believe to be good for themselves, they suffer in two ways. Death, jail, and imprisonment are the extreme consequence, particularly with a change in political regime. The psychological consequences revealed to us by Covid, particularly in children, and the exponential increase in mental health problems are the latter.

From the lockdowns, how many Covid deaths were prevented? The number fluctuates from zero to 0.02%.

As early as April 2021, the European Journal of Clinical Investigation published a review of the stay-at-home orders and mandatory business closures' efficacy in reducing the spread of Covid. Using standard research methods, here is their conclusion:

> In summary, we fail to find strong evidence supporting a role for more restrictive NPIs [nonpharmacological interventions] in the control of COVID in early 2020. We do not question the role of all public health interventions, or of coordinated communications about the epidemic, but we fail to find an additional benefit of stay-at-home orders and business closures. The data cannot fully exclude the possibility of some benefits. However, even if they exist, these benefits may not match the numerous harms of these aggressive measures. More targeted public health interventions that more effectively reduce transmissions may

be important for future epidemic control without the harms of highly restrictive measures. (2021)

They also noted:

> Empirical data for the characteristics of fatalities in the later wave before mrNPIs [more restrictive non-pharmacological interventions] were adopted as compared with the first wave (when mrNPIs had been used) show that the proportion of COVID-19 deaths that occurred in nursing homes was *often higher under mrNPIs* rather than under less-restrictive measures. (2021, emphasis added)

The publication also highlighted "coordinated communications about the epidemic." The censorship by government and big tech contributed to the confusion and heated disagreements among agencies throughout the catastrophe.

Nearly four years following the onset of the 2020 public restrictions, Meta CEO, Mark Zuckerberg stated that "it was improper for the Biden administration to have pressured Facebook to censor content in 2021 related to the coronavirus pandemic, vowing that the social-media giant would reject any such future efforts" (Siobhan Hughes, WSJ, 2024).

More insidious are the subtle consequences. This is where impact cannot be exactly pinpointed because we never know what could have been. Of the projected 100 million recently dead, who could have cured cancer? Of the 100 million from the last century, who could have mass-produced water from air we breathe? Or invented teleportation? Or interstellar travel?

I'm sure my imagination cannot fathom the full magnitude of loss. Experts in the field, like Dr. Bhattacharya, also noted that school closures, stay-at-home mandates, and business closures were not part of the prior-established protocol. This issue is indicative of the problems that arise when one or a handful of unelected experts, who refuse to listen to those closest to the problem, insist on directing the actions of many. Even the term "health czar" illustrates the inappropriate level of power one person possessed at the time.

Experts, by definition, only have a myopic, ever-shrinking sliver of perspective into the lives of most people. By definition, in fact, as an expert increases their knowledge of a subject, they actually learn less about everything else. Only the people who live their own lives know what is truly best for themselves on a macro scale. An individual, over a period of time, is an expert on their life. Thus, the implicit knowledge about subtle differences between themselves and others are the very nuances that may save lives in an emergency.

Experts will tell you that sending 1.3 million manufacturing jobs to Mexico is best for the consumer and the Mexican worker. Experts agreed that economic policy embracing a communist nation's slave labor force and exporting nearly five million manufacturing jobs is best for the end user. Prices are lowered and standards in China were improved. After all, we are a global economy now.

Please detect the sarcasm here. Small business in the US have suffered greatly at the decisions of experts, elected and otherwise.

It is worth noting that the CCP has killed more people than any other political regime in known world history. Communism, by definition, dictates what its people do, where they work, and for how much. The lifestyle improvements of the few in China's major cities are only at the whim of the CCP. This depresses the value of labor and does not reflect the actual cost of its exports.

The surplus generated has given the CCP incredible economic power worldwide. Americans and the west *may* get a cheaper iPhone, but we only risk enslaving more of the world—and perhaps ourselves—in the very near future. The suffering of those who exist under that regime is without measure.

Business owners and the policymakers for whom they funded elections are responsible for the hollowing out of America. Entertain my hyperbole here for a moment. Just in my lifetime, as the blue-collar dads of the 70s and 80s became unemployed, they became alcoholics, their children became drug addicts, and their grandchildren have now become masters at manipulating the welfare system for benefits. These meager benefits will never create a standard of living worth embracing. Hopelessness is all they can look forward to. The American military has lowered its physical fitness entrance standards because children are no longer raised to be active, but rather join dad—if he's present—in the man-cave to play video games and binge-watch video streaming.

Overstatement?

Maybe, maybe not. The military strength of the US is not only dependent on the fitness of its soldiers, but the sourcing of its weapons. America's industrial base has been decimated by offshore manufacturing. We've either forgotten or don't have the capacity to make a thing.

Not a coincidence to them, but comical and sad to me, is that the CCP is an imminent threat to us and our allies in the Pacific. Yet, they make a significant amount of parts for our war submarines.

> **America has forgotten how, or lacks the capacity, from a shrinking skilled labor market, to make a thing**

According to the *Wall Street Journal*, America has a budget of around 2.5 per year, but they supply us with parts at a rate of 1.5 per year. This is no accident, yet our policymakers change nothing.

Why would the CCP threaten these institutions?

While we continue to argue over skin color and gender-affirming bathrooms, they are outpacing our military manufacturing three to one. They don't care if we ever decide on gender, equity, or any other argument. They want us distracted by North Korea, Russia, and Iran while they use our hyper-consumer money to build up. With no manufacturing base, and munitions going to these small conflicts, we have no way to stop them from controlling the western Pacific. Our allies, Japan, Taiwan, South Korea, Malaysia and Australia, do not stand a chance.

In his book, *Getting China Wrong*, Aaron L. Friedberg examines in detail the mistakes western business leaders and policy makers have made in the last few decades. He writes:

> Instead of moving steadily toward greater openness and more reliance on markets, as most observers predicted and expected, Beijing has expanded its use of state-directed trade, technology promotion, and industrial policies. Despite the Chinese Communist Party (CCP) regime's ceaseless rhetoric about the glories of globalization and the wonders of "win-win cooperation," these policies now threaten the future prosperity of the advanced industrial nations... Rather than loosen up, the Chinese party-state has cracked down on its own citizens, stifling the slightest hint of dissent, laying the foundations for a pervasive, nationwide high-tech surveillance system, and consigning at least a million of the country's Uighur Muslims to forced labor and concentration camps. China today is more repressive than at any time since the 1989 Tiananmen Square massacre and arguably since the Cultural Revolution of the 1960s.

As much of the CCP's political documentation and long-term planning has revealed, their goal was never most favored nation status. They are masters at hinting at a direction and letting their enemies move that way. It has never been about trade and prosperity, only global dominance. One only needs to observe how the CCP treated Hong Kong in the years that followed its reunion with mainland China to know what their intentions are for other free states.

Regarding sustainable energy, they never acquiesced to follow agreed upon rules or followed them when they did agree. As icing on the proverbial cake, Chinese technology monitors US ports. This runaway train presents the most obvious military threat.

An article released by the *Christian Post* in 2011 revealed that the CCP held Christian values as the foundation for America, Britain, and Western Europe's economic success. It also noted that the CCP is well-aware of Christianity's ability to defeat other communist systems throughout the world.

Undermining Christian values in the west has proven to be the most strategic initiative the CCP has ever embraced. Jerry Newcombe from *The Christian Post* published a more recent article in 2023 titled, "The greatest story ever distorted: China rewriting the Bible?" which details the CCP's effort to completely undermine the Christian faith and future followers in China and its affiliates. He writes:

> A powerful story of forgiveness is found in John 8, involving Jesus and the woman caught in adultery, wherein He famously said, "Let him who is without sin cast the first stone." Her accusers quietly leave, one after another. Jesus then tells her that neither does He accuse her, "But go and sin no more"—a part often ignored today by our *tolerant* society. But now, if the Chinese Communists have their way, the whole story of Jesus and the adulterous woman will be completely turned on its head. In their version, Jesus Himself stones her to death!

This adulteration of our Lord's earthly ministry is not surprising, given the CCP's murderous infiltration into all walks of Chinese life. From an interview with US Congressman Mike Gallagher, Newcombe quotes the statesman:

> It isn't enough that the Chinese Communists have burned many Scriptures. It isn't enough that they actively ban the Bible online through firewalls on social media outlets. Now, apparently they dare to attempt to destroy it from within, by rewriting it. Gallagher comments: "Across Henan province, local CCP officials forced Protestant churches to replace the Ten Commandments with Xi Jinping quotes. 'Thou shalt have no other gods before Me,' became diktats like: 'Resolutely guard against the infiltration of Western ideology.'" Today's Chinese Communists are following in the footsteps of Chairman Mao, the worst mass-murderer in the history of the world, who called religion "poison." And the Chinese Communists persecute all religions.

What is the alternative? Where does the shift need to take place?

Faith. Regardless of your background or doctrine, faith is the propellant to the future. Leaders don't always know if their decisions about life and business are correct. They believe a thing and take corresponding action.

> **Regardless of your background or doctrine, faith is the propellant to the future**

Without faith, one is doomed to a current reality that is ever-changing and unmanageable, shifting with each new wind of so-called science and clever version of dictatorial rule.

Faith doesn't allow us to control our reality per se. Faith allows us only two things. First, we make up our mind about a given set of facts. Then we believe an outcome toward the future, based on our mindset. We capture our emotions concerning that outcome to prevent being tossed around by every event that may set itself against said belief and corresponding decisions. To summarize, you can only control two things, your attitude and your actions. But if those two components are aligned with a set of facts, then your likelihood of success in the future, however unknown it may be, increases dramatically.

The science behind alignment of attitude and action can be found in the Big 5 or Five Factor Model personality assessment. Through the data collected, statistically that is, those who are optimistic toward the future have greater success professionally. By that definition, these individuals are considered high in extroversion. The Jungian definition of extroversion is somewhat different, but still involves an attraction to others, outside activities, and ideas. One who is slightly okay with engaging others will increase their success and happiness in life. The Christian faith's primary goal brings alignment of our attitudes and actions toward others with a singular focus. Go and make disciples.

As leaders, we cannot overlook the need to help others achieve their goals while in the pursuit of our own. To look beyond yourself for a cause, a group of people, and a power greater than yourself, brings to life the concept of faith in both business and our personal lives.

As I've noted, in my consulting organization, *iNTREPiD iMPACT Team*, and *Jerry Howard International* as a whole, faith, leadership, and business are as inseparable as Father, Son, and Holy Spirit. Remember, you can't have business without people, you can't have people without leadership, and you can't have leadership without control of your attitude and actions around an agreed upon doctrine of faith. Faith in business causes us to look beyond experts and into the hearts of our people.

There are many reasons—and not just fiscal gains—as to why the west embraced the CCP, but disengagement will be a significant financial hurdle. However, those who proclaim it as a global catastrophe, fail to recall the enormous strength of a politically favorable democratic society when build up is called for. Both during and after WWII, America, Europe and post-war Japan recovered from far worse. In chapter two we learned that easy access to capital, reduced bureaucracy, and favorable policy can radically change a society in less than a decade.

What if, fifty years ago, instead of drooling over the profit potential from China's enslaved workforce, we worked to undermine the CCP's exploitation of the Chinese population?

We should have set *those* captives free. In our faith, the Chinese people deserve democracy and to live in prosperity. In recent conflicts, namely those in the Middle East, we learned that setting up a democratic system *for* someone doesn't work.

How can we train them to seek that outcome for themselves? Faith. God's word. What if we doused China's society with faith-driven literature and opened up faith-based social networks to its people?

> The irony in the CCP's strategy for us to finance our own annihilation cannot be overlooked. Satan did the same thing to Adam and Eve

It's the same tactic for which the CCP uses TikTok and why they give billions of dollars to our legacy academic institutions. We indirectly funded their rise to near global dominance. The irony in the CCP's strategy for us to finance our own annihilation cannot be overlooked. Satan did the same thing to Adam and Eve!

Although many decades have passed, the CCP consistently controls the population through many institutions, mostly digital. Philosophically, control is rooted in a kind of rhetorical fear of bringing back their great humiliation, civil war, and even the enormous death toll of Mao's revolution. Today, control is deployed through social constrictions, community shame, and economic limitations on those who don't comply. Jail, torture, and execution are still used when necessary.

We should be postulating what we can do to their systems. American businessmen abandoned the primary goal of our faith: "go and make disciples." Instead of embracing the CCP's economic goals, we should have conspired to help them embrace ours.

The mission of Jesus is "go and make disciples." The vision is that all people of the earth receive salvation through Him and join the family. His values are: love God, and love others as you love yourself. This is the agreed upon doctrine of the faith that made America and the west so prosperous.

The CCP suspected that forty years ago, researched it twenty years ago, and still knows it. Yet we abandoned it in the marketplace and eroded the fabric of our own society. In another generation, maybe two, their system will be the only one to choose. Submit to us or die of starvation. It worked for Stalin.

Faith-driven leaders must follow God's blueprint for world-class business. This free-market system built around Judeo-Christian values not only guarantees that we win without massive bloodshed, but the world prospers with us. We were the leaders before, and we can lead again. Business in America is the nation's largest mission field. Its people yearn for a cause greater than themselves to bring meaning to their work.

In an interview on the international podcast *Faith Driven Entrepreneur*, Jason Honescko with David Kinnaman from the Barna group reported that 6 percent of people in America trusted Congress. No surprise there. They also stated that only 32 percent trust the church. That was far lower than I would have expected. However, what gave me great hope was that 61 percent of people trust small business (2024)!

This is where real impact is possible. It makes sense too. Rebecca Leppert, from the Pew Research Center, reported that the US consists of approximately six million small businesses that have employees. Small business owners employ more people than any other type in the country. They also serve their communities, not just with goods and services, but as leaders in local organizations and offices. They have to be fair and honest—their customers and constituents are their neighbors!

I devoted most of this chapter discussing the CCP because other than our own acquiescence, it is the number one threat to worldwide freedom and prosperity. I intentionally make a clear distinction between the CCP and China's general population. Many of them hold extreme disdain for the CCP and risk their lives daily to lead Christian organizations.

Faith-driven leaders have a golden opportunity to turn the tide of wokeism and CCP influence right here in our neighborhoods. Bring back manufacturing and decentralize the resources of communities to their local governments to pre-1930 levels.

So far, we've examined what and why we need faith-driven leaders and world-class business. The how of implementation is closer to home than you might think and will be the focus of the remaining content.

Remember, people don't change because of the talking heads. They watch what validates their beliefs. People change their minds when their friends and community leaders share their time, skills, and income with them. They change when we invest in their kids' futures. They follow when our passion is implanted in their hearts through good works. Implementing first principles with *The Big Ten for Business* will begin the transformation to truly love God and love people!

The Boardroom or Bible Study

For group discussion and individual journaling:

How does the freedom to govern your personal life relate to business or economic freedom? Why?

Why is it important to have a leader who is subordinated to God and the people they serve?

How has the shrinking of America's vocational labor force impacted your family?

How does faith determine the future trajectory of everyone, even the unsaved?

How do the world's enemies to freedom use the same tactics as Satan in the garden?

PART III

HOW TO, FOR YOU: BECOMING A FAITH-DRIVEN LEADER

Search me, O God, and know my heart; test me and know my anxious thoughts. Point out anything in me that offends you, and lead me along the path of everlasting life.

-Psalm 139:23-24

CHAPTER 8

THE BIG TEN FOR BUSINESS: WHO'S REALLY IN CHARGE

> "Your attitude, not your aptitude, will determine your altitude."
> –Zig Ziglar

As a follower of the way of Jesus Christ, business leaders must consider God's values. If you believe God wrote the story of your life, then it's His story, His guidelines. Easy said, but without humility, difficult to execute. Remember:

> You [God] saw me before I was born.
> Every day of my life was recorded in your book.
> Every moment was laid out
> before a single day had passed. (Ps. 139:16)

Under this assumption, our desires originate from Him. Thus, pursuit of Him is pursuit of our aspirations. It cannot be the other way around. He comes first. With and through Him, we realize them with joy and peace.

When was the last time you had both?

The Big Ten for Business, God's ten commandments or statements, are your path to three things: a purpose for existence, a process to follow, and power to execute.

The oft quoted, "But seek first the kingdom of God and His righteousness, and all these things shall be added to you …" is a great summary, but we need more actionable guidance (Matt. 6:33 NKJV). Christians who write off the Old Testament get hung up here because of that very problem.

What's your interpretation?

At one point mine was, *All the material things I want to show others God loves me will be added to me so I can relax with joy and be at peace with no toil and* … you get the point. Stated as such, it is much easier to realize the bad, "name it, claim it," doctrine. Taken out of context, that scripture has inadvertently led millions of Christians away from God's true call on their lives. Pointing a finger at God, they feel as though He didn't uphold His end of the contract.

Taking a closer look, Jesus commands us to seek first His kingdom (Renner, 2019). This is not optional. Following that, we act with righteousness. Through His process of sanctification, we come to know His perfect purpose for us. Then, and only then, everything we need to carry that mission is "added to [us]."

You might be thinking, "Jerry, what about money?"

The *power* includes all the *provision* you'll need to succeed—plus an overflow to bless others. Recall when Jesus fed the multitudes:

> Then he told the people to sit down on the grass. Jesus took the *five loaves and two fish*, looked up toward heaven, and blessed them.

Then, breaking the loaves into pieces, he gave the bread to the disciples, who distributed it to the people. They all ate as much as they wanted, and afterward, the disciples picked up *twelve baskets of leftovers*. About 5,000 men were fed that day, in addition to all the women and children! (Matt. 14:19-21, emphasis added)

Jesus had a *purpose* for the meager amount of fish and loaves. He followed a *process* of gratitude. Through the *power* of God's kingdom, he had more than enough *provision* to execute the miracle—with an overflow remaining! It was the Lord's faith, captured in the Holy Spirit, that activated it all. Your faith, even if only as small as a mustard seed, partnered with God's spirit in you, while following God's guidelines for life, will do the same. Believe it or not, you can have the same impact when you operate God's way. Jesus is CEO, you are the operator.

> **Jesus had purpose, process, power, and provision**

Let's imagine that Moses was something *like a god* to the Hebrews through the eternal God's empowerment. And Joshua, who led them to the promised land, is what I call a forward-looking reflection of Jesus, who leads us to His eternal promised land.

From a business perspective, consider Joshua as Chief Operating Officer for the Jewish nation. Originally, he was Moses' assistant, easily translated as Chief of Staff. Upon Moses' death, God anoints Joshua as His direct report, promises to keep him safe and repeatedly orders him to "Be strong and courageous ..." (Josh. 1:6). In addition, God gave him specific instructions on how to stay under protection and how to be strong and courageous. He specifies here:

> Be strong and very courageous. Be careful to obey all the instructions Moses gave you. Do not deviate from them, turning either to the right or to the left. Then you will be successful in everything you do. Study this Book of Instruction *continually*. Meditate on it *day and night* so you will be sure to *obey* everything written in it. Only then will you *prosper and succeed* in all you do. (Josh. 1:7-8, emphasis added)

God reminds him success requires process.

How many business books provide ten steps to wealth? Five steps to power? Twenty-one ways to scale? Why would we think our faith is any different?

Again, our old friend, complacency. The intangible drives the tangible, but because we cannot see it, we forget.

There were 613 laws governing the Jewish culture. Initially, God started with ten, the Ten Commandments, or ten "statements" as they were considered in the original Jewish language. The statements are the foundation for following the "Book of Instruction." Everything in business hinges on these same principles.

Look at the Gospel according to John and imagine Jesus at the end of his earthly ministry.

> When Jesus had tasted it, he said, "It is finished!" Then he bowed his head and gave up his spirit. (John 19:30)

"It is finished" was Jesus' indicator to God and man that the laws of the Old Covenant had been completely fulfilled here on earth. Then he descended into hell for three days to proclaim the same to all the principalities and powers in the unseen places. Peter gives more detail in his epistle:

> Christ suffered for our sins once for all time. He never sinned, but he died for sinners to bring you safely home to God. He suffered physical

> death, but he was raised to life in the Spirit. So he went and *preached to the spirits in prison*—those who disobeyed God long ago when God waited patiently while Noah was building his boat. (1 Pet. 3:18-20, emphasis added)

All law has been fulfilled, but there are some nuances that need to be considered before writing off the Old Testament completely.

Some Christians today will assert that the Ten Commandments, because they are a part of the Old Covenant, are no longer applicable. It is true that Jesus went to the cross and started the New Covenant. By doing so, He fulfilled all of Jewish law—all 613 of them. A few, he not only fulfilled, but *elevated* (Stells, J., personal communications, 2021). *Elevated* means he emphasized their importance, reinforced their relevance, and established them as perpetual functions of the soul, not just matters to be executed outwardly. Thus, the origins of the Old Covenant are just as relevant as before the cross.

Reference Joshua, our Old Testament model for chief steward of God's people, and something *like a Christ*. Even he and Jesus' names in Hebrew are identical, Yehoshua (Joshua), although we use the Greek translation, Iesous (Jesus). *The Big Ten for Business*, or Ten Commandments worked for Joshua, and Jesus maintained their importance in His teaching. An easy conclusion to draw is that they are exactly what business leaders need. They are a decision-making guide for our personal lives and should be echoed outward throughout our organizations.

If God's Mission, or *Missio Dei*, is for us to "therefore, go and make disciples of all the nations ..." and part of His vision is "in the future you will see the Son of Man seated in the place of power at God's right hand and coming on the clouds of heaven," then the Big Ten are His value statements (Matt. 28:19, Matt. 26:64).

In *The Big Ten for Business*, we are going to remove the "Do Not…" and state what action to take. We will reveal in each statement where Jesus and the New Testament church elevates the moral law. We will also look at how it ensures the effective operation of a business.

Keep in mind, the first five get our heart and mind in alignment, or attitude I like to say, and the last five determine how we interact with others. God starts off in this manner:

> Then God gave the people all these instructions: "I am the LORD your God, who rescued you from the land of Egypt, the place of your slavery. "You must not have any other god but me." (Exod. 20:1-3).

Recall that the Ten Commandments were originally written as "words" or "statements" (Prager, 2018). The first "commandment" is actually two statements. This is why, when questioned by the teacher of the law, Jesus started with "the Lord your God is the one and only Lord" (Mark 12:29). It is important to remember that He is the Rescuer, and all other gods are false. Then God states what not to do. "You must not have any other god but me" (Exod. 20:3).

WORSHIP GOD ONLY

As an actionable phrase, we could rightly say, WORSHIP GOD ONLY. Very simple and easy to remember. In the west, we don't think of worshiping other gods as was traditionally done, but our preoccupation with the planet, money, skin tone, and gender are certainly taking a front seat in the car God should be driving. Elevated in the New Covenant, we read:

> Jesus replied, "What does the law of Moses say? How do you read it?" The man answered, "'You must love the LORD your God with all your heart, all your soul, all your strength, and all your mind. And love your

neighbor as yourself.'" "Right!" Jesus told him. "Do this and you will live!" (Luke 10:26-28)

My favorite way to remember this in business is, Jesus is CEO. If you are the boss, He is the boss of you. Let's see how that came about:

In the beginning, *God created* the heavens and *the earth*. (Gen. 1:1, emphasis added)

That appears to cover your house and business. Skipping ahead a few verses:

Then *God* looked over all *he had made*, and he saw that it was very good! (Gen. 1:31, emphasis added)

It is definitive who is in command. If not, in the establishment of the New Covenant, John's Gospel declares the same:

JESUS IS CEO

In the beginning the Word already existed. The Word was with God, and the Word was God. He existed in the beginning with God. *God created everything through him*, and *nothing was created except through him*. (John 1:1-3, emphasis added)

Both God in Genesis and the Apostle John explicitly reveal that everything was made *by* Him and *through* Him. Thus, Jesus owns it all. Here's how the Psalmist describes it:

For all the animals of the forest are mine,
and I own the cattle on a thousand hills.
I know every bird on the mountains,
and all the animals of the field are mine.

> If I were hungry, I would not tell you,
> for all *the world is mine and everything in it.*
> (Ps. 50:10-12, emphasis added)

God is not mincing words here. "The world is [His] and everything in it!" If Jesus is CEO, that makes you and I operators, not owners.

If I hired you to run one of my companies, don't you think it would it be a good idea to check in with me about what is to be done?

I would at least require you to learn the mission to be carried out and the vision of where we are going. To stay employed, only decisions based on the company's values would be tolerated.

Brings a new perspective to our lofty positions and titles, doesn't it?

In my first six months as a new hospital executive, I didn't make decisions. First, I spent six weeks in the boardroom learning the broad strokes. Then, I was on site for another five months getting my hours for licensure. Only after passing the test did I get assigned as interim CEO somewhere under close supervision. Those were only contract assignments until I was assigned something permanent. That first year was spent learning how to do the job for which I was called. Upon that calling, I had to submit to the mission, vision, and values of the company.

Today, submission is not often celebrated. One wrong but commonly held belief is, "if it is to be, it's up to me." This may hurt, but that statement is a lie from the pit of hell. I know its intent. Saying it helps to get us off the couch. Although those of us who aren't typically on the couch probably don't need that to get something done.

I'm not perfect; I've wasted plenty of time in my life on drugs, alcohol, fornication, porn, you name it. Under the Lordship of Jesus, it took countless hours of study and prayer to rid myself of those habits. Simultaneously, I had to rid myself of the belief that it was up to me. Numerous leaders in the SMB are cursed under that lie.

> **Positioning Jesus as CEO, we accept that some things, most things, are not in our control**

To truly see His work in my life, and my role in it, I had to subordinate my will to His. Positioning Jesus as CEO and our thinking from a lower place, we accept that some things—most things—are simply not in our control. The level of peace in this posture is priceless. Furthermore, under Him, we get to tap into God's resources, insights and abilities. God was the first and is still the number one venture capitalist for humans!

Up next, God's second value statement reads this way:

> You must not make for yourself an idol of any kind or an image of anything in the heavens or on the earth or in the sea. (Exod. 20:4)

God makes it clear that there is *nothing* in heaven (other than He), or on earth or in the sea that can represent Him appropriately or accurately. Hard as we may try, nothing can effectively replace Him in our lives, either.

Related to His first value statement, God establishes himself as supreme. He further requires us not to carve anything out of wood or stone and bow down to it. Through the prophet Isaiah, God illustrates how silly that practice is:

> He burns part of the tree to roast his meat and to keep himself warm. He says, "Ah, that fire feels good." Then he takes what's left and makes his god: a carved idol! He falls down in front of it, worshiping and praying to it. "Rescue me!" he says. "You are my god!" Such stupidity

and ignorance! Their eyes are closed, and they cannot see. Their minds are shut, and they cannot think. The person who made the idol never stops to reflect, "Why, it's just a block of wood!" (Isa. 44:16-19)

Do we ever stop to think, it's just a ... car, truck, house, job, career, business. Fill in the blank with your idol. I've worshiped all manner of idols—even after becoming a Christian!

First, I worshiped making six figures. Then I idolized being an executive. Once I got my first CEO job, then I wanted a bigger budget, then more staff, then more profit so I could max out the bonus. After buying my first business, I wanted another one, bought that, then a bigger budget, and more staff! On and on, I was never fulfilled!

How arrogant (and typical) of me to pray God's word to Him, thinking I was being pious and obedient. My mouth spoke his words, while my heart and intentions broke every one of His value statements.

What does the New Testament say about submitting to the will of God?

Luke details how Paul addresses the Athenians:

> For in him we live and move and exist. As some of your own poets have said, 'We are his offspring.' And since this is true, we shouldn't think of God as an idol designed by craftsmen from gold or silver or stone. (Acts 17:28-29)

FOLLOW TRUTH

You are God's son and daughter. He is not a magic lamp you rub when you need your profit and loss statement to look better. As a child of the *Most High God*, everything that is His, is ours. We must play by His rules and give reverence where it's due. His plan for your life is infinitely more incredible than you can imagine—and it extends into eternity!

Our action statement also works in business. God's second rule for life is simply, FOLLOW TRUTH. God is truth, and His word is a direct representation and manifestation of Him in this universe. As John said, "The Word was *with* God, and the Word *was* God" (John 1:1, emphasis added). But Jesus said it best:

> During that time the devil came and said to him, "If you are the Son of God, tell these stones to become loaves of bread." But Jesus told him, "No! The Scriptures say, 'People do not live by bread alone, but by every word that comes from the mouth of God'" (Matt. 4:3-4)

I love this for the second commandment because not only does Jesus prioritize God's word, but He ignores the devil's implication that He might *not* be the Son of God. Satan will start there with you as well. He convinced Eve in the garden:

> "You won't die!" the serpent replied to the woman. "God knows that your eyes will be opened as soon as you eat it, and you will be like God, knowing both good and evil." The woman was convinced. She saw that the tree was beautiful and its fruit looked delicious, and she wanted the wisdom it would give her" (Gen. 3:4-6)

The enemy knows our weakness is rooted in dependency. That is why, despite titles or positions, you are not CEO. We have a God-sized hole in our soul that only Jesus can fill. When we forget who we are (sons and daughters of the Most High God) and to whom we belong (God's chosen people, special and holy), we seek things of this world to meet our needs instead of Him.

What about part two of God's second statement for life? Let's read:

> "I lay the sins of the parents upon their children; the entire family is affected—even children in the third and fourth generations of those

who reject me. But I lavish unfailing love for a thousand generations on those who love me and obey my commands." (Exod. 20:5-6)

I used to interpret that as a dark warning about God's wrath on children due to the sins of their parents. Jesus dispelled that when he explained to his disciples:

"It was not because of his sins or his parents' sins," Jesus answered. "This happened so the power of God could be seen in him." (John 9:3)

For me, it helped to perceive God's directive as the urgent guidance of a loving father. In my mind God was saying, "Hey, in this mountainous terrain of life, you must walk along this exact path, step only where I tell you to, *follow every word in this book of instruction*, or you and your family will fall off a cliff!"

When we do not heed the word of God, we walk right off the proverbial cliff, taking everyone with us! The long-term effect of disobedience and following the world's idols on the third and fourth generations is bitterness, envy, strife.

How many churches have crumbled from bad doctrine? Or the senior pastor running off with a girlfriend?

Personally, learning to obey God's will helped me to prioritize life in this order: faith, family, finances. If you put God first, the family gets appropriate leadership. When you put family over finances, you show up in the workplace, church, and community as your best self. That solidifies your reputation to others. Pursue God, your family, the world, in that order.

In His Old Testament commands, God was foreshadowing Jesus. The effect of Jesus on the generations that follow His influence—should they continue to follow Him—are both abundant and eternal, "for a thousand generations." When you make Jesus CEO and follow truth, your eyes behold what is best. Everything else falls in place, *without* curse or toil.

The Boardroom or Bible Study

For group discussion and individual journaling:

What enabled Jesus to manifest enough food for the 5,000? How can you do the same in your life?

What are three things, other than God, that you worship? Why do they get first priority?

Whether you lead a team or not, own a business or not, what does "Jesus is CEO" mean to you?

What are three things that you try to control, but fail? Why do you try? Why does it fail?

What does it mean to "Follow Truth?" Where have you seen that produce fruit? When does it cause turmoil?

CHAPTER 9

THE BIG TEN FOR BUSINESS: WORDS AND RHYTHM

"He that can take rest is greater than he that can take cities."
–Benjamin Franklin

As Christian business people, we are His image bearers. As a leader, you have a *duty of care* to those under your charge. Simply put, you need to act right. Practice is the process. Paul teaches the church at Corinth:

> This means that anyone who belongs to Christ has become a new person. The old life is gone; a new life has begun! (2 Cor. 5:17)

As a new creation, you represent your God, yourself, your family, your company, and most importantly all of us Believers out here trying to shine the light of Jesus. So make it count! To do so, the third value statement God wants us to follow reads this way:

> You must not misuse the name of the LORD your God. The LORD will not let you go unpunished if you misuse his name. (Exod. 20:7)

It is as serious as it looks.

Using the Lord's name in vain has been misunderstood for many years. Here's what I learned. If improperly followed, this command can lead to the worst of punishment. Most people think of this as saying, "God d**n a thing." But God has never damned anything. For starters, saying that is simply a lie.

Satan loves to damn things, or cause them to be under the curse, particularly us. His name, Ha'Satan means adversary, or accuser. Thus, when a person says "g"—"d" a thing or situation, they are merely calling Satan god, which he enjoys greatly. Assigning authority of that situation to Satan is a label he gladly accepts.

Truly using the Lord's name in vain starts with His actual name. YHWH has no known pronunciation in Hebrew or English. We say Yahweh for simplicity, and the letters to build that name are Yod-Hey-Vav-Hey. "God" is His title (Prager, 2022).

More specifically, when we enter into an oath or covenant under His name, breaking that oath reflects poorly on Him. His righteous nature cannot allow a poor reflection, which is why it is number three on the list. God will not forgive a person who does evil things in His name.

What does Jesus have to say about that?

He agrees, of course! When elevated to the New Covenant, Jesus made it simple:

> You have also heard that our ancestors were told, 'You must not break your vows; you must carry out the vows you make to the LORD.' But I say, do not make any vows! Do not say, 'By heaven!' because heaven

is God's throne. And do not say, 'By the earth!' because the earth is his footstool. And do not say, 'By Jerusalem!' for Jerusalem is the city of the great King. Do not even say, 'By my head!' for you can't turn one hair white or black. Just say a simple, 'Yes, I will,' or 'No, I won't.' Anything beyond this is from the evil one. (Matt. 5:33-37)

"Yes, I will," or "No, I won't." How relaxing. Jesus is clear that anything more than that is from our enemy. He's not messing around here. A terrorist shedding innocent blood in God's name will not be able to stand before God's judgment. A priest carrying out acts of molestation with children is another example of those committing evil in God's name. Operating in God's name is a position of authority and has a higher standard here and in eternity. Consequently, the penalty magnifies.

> **WORDS HAVE POWER**

What can we do with this in business? Remember this: WORDS HAVE POWER. If God used words to create the heavens and the earth and gave us authority to reign and replenish, we cannot speak idly.

Every business owner and leader should ensure their words represent an actual reality or future that others can depend upon. Leaders build trust through consistency and acting ethically, abiding by their founding principles, especially when it's *inconvenient*. Making empty promises in the name of the company, issuing false or manipulative statements, and practicing any form of dishonesty should be avoided at all costs.

Every memo, contract, email, and conversation has meaning. Not unlike political offices, in leadership our words can be interpreted as policy. We are held to account for the consequences of our words. Use only the minimum number of words needed to convey your point. Remember, not everyone thinks or sees the world the way you do.

Further, God's fourth value statement is incredibly important to business. You've probably heard it many times, and like me, have probably failed to follow it. Here's what He says:

> Remember to observe the Sabbath day by keeping it holy. You have six days each week for your ordinary work, but the seventh day is a Sabbath day of rest dedicated to the LORD your God. (Exod. 20:8-10a)

He begins by indicating that ordinary work, that which sustains you and your family, was to include enough effort to cover our needs through the seventh day. He also implies that those days' purpose is to point to the Holy day. God wants us to work toward life, not that life is merely for work (Prager, 2022). He gets very specific afterward:

> On that day no one in your household may do any work. This includes you, your sons and daughters, your male and female servants, your livestock, and any foreigners living among you. For in six days the LORD made the heavens, the earth, the sea, and everything in them; but on the seventh day he rested. That is why the LORD blessed the Sabbath day and set it apart as holy. (Exod. 20:10b–11)

There is no other record in history where foreigners, servants, and even livestock were required to rest.

Under God, this gave slaves a kind of equality with their Jewish masters, also never before seen in human history. I will note that Jewish law brought many more "firsts" of how humans are to interact with one another, much of which is taken for granted today, but that is beyond the scope of this book. My goal is to lead you to God's word and a deeper understanding of its relevance to life and especially work.

How does Jesus elevate the Sabbath?

Many would argue that he fights against the Sabbath being holy. He does many good works on the Sabbath, but clarifies its place:

> Jesus replied, "Haven't you read in the Scriptures what David did when he and his companions were hungry? He went into the house of God and broke the law by eating the sacred loaves of bread that only the priests can eat. He also gave some to his companions." And Jesus added, "The Son of Man is *Lord, even over the Sabbath.*" (Luke 6:3-5, emphasis added)

As Lord, He owns the Sabbath just as everything else in the universe. He created the Sabbath for us to rest. Jesus went on to rebuke those who would accuse Him of breaking the law:

> But Jesus knew their thoughts. He said to the man with the deformed hand, "Come and stand in front of everyone." So the man came forward. Then Jesus said to his critics, "I have a question for you. Does the law permit good deeds on the Sabbath, or is it a day for doing evil? Is this a day to save life or to destroy it?" (Luke 6:8-9)

These passages are often misconstrued to indicate the Sabbath is no longer important. However, none of us are Lord or beyond physical, emotional, and spiritual decay. We need rest. We need healing. We need peace. Luke details Jesus' perspective here:

> But the Lord replied, "You hypocrites! Each of you works on the Sabbath day! Don't you untie your ox or your donkey from its stall on the Sabbath and lead it out for water? This dear woman, a daughter of Abraham, has been held in bondage by Satan for eighteen years. *Isn't it right that she be released, even on the Sabbath?*" This shamed his enemies, but all the people rejoiced at the wonderful things he did. (Luke 13:15-17, emphasis added)

Healing and being released from bondage, or the slavery of constant work, is holy!

In the New Covenant, we worship on Sunday, the first day of the week to both celebrate the risen King, but also to give our first fruits of time to gathering together with other Believers. This is Holy work. God inhabits the praises of His people, so I can think of no better way to start the week!

The Hebrews followed Genesis on a night, then day, rhythm. It reminds us that God always goes from less to more, or dark to light, never the other way around. The Sabbath, or Shabbat, begins Friday at sundown for them. Jesus rose with the sun on the third day, so the perspective changed a bit for Christians.

> **REST WEEKLY: PRAISE—PERFORM—PRAY**

Many of us still rest on Saturday. If Sunday is for worship, then Saturday should be for family, which is more like the original Shabbat custom. Extra prayer with family on Saturday would be a nice way to round out the week. Bookend your week with prayer and family!

PRAISE—PERFORM—PRAY. One day for worship, five days for ordinary work, one day for prayer. This has so many levels of benefit, but here are a few. By taking a few days of rest, you are admitting your humanity and, in effect, modeling a bit of humility for those around you. People need rest, even the most driven cannot get to the mountaintop alone. Thus, the team members, regardless of the superhuman tenacity of some leaders, need to recharge weekly.

I was in a position similar to COO early in my executive healthcare career. The current CEO, a godly Christian woman who I still highly respect, told me that she once worked thirty days straight. Although appalled, to remain coachable, I inquired. Motivated by guilt for asking her leadership team to work weekends, she said it was to show them she was not above putting in the hours as well. Sounds noble, but I knew she was headed for disaster.

Two years later and near a nervous breakdown, she resigned and left the industry. After many years away, she recharged, refocused her faith, and got married. Thankfully, she did return to her true calling in life as a hospital executive, with her priorities in order. Faith, Family, Finances. We are friends and colleagues to this day.

In addition to learning how to build a great team and hire first-rate players, Mr. Cartwright, the first executive mentor I had and my favorite faith-driven leader, required us to "figure out how to run the center in fifty hours or less." This was exciting to me, because it meant that I had permission to be human! Ten-hour days I didn't mind, but with four kids, two of whom were in diapers back then, I needed my weekends.

By the time I was in my fifth year, my team and I worked with diligence and efficiency, rarely exceeding forty hours. It was no coincidence that center consistently exceeded the quarterly budgeted profit goals and was given the coveted five-star crown for clinical outcomes. The patients were healing, and the business was incredibly lucrative.

The secret was we all recognized our humanity, recharged effectively, and brought our absolute best. You cannot bring your best beyond fifty-five hours of work per week. Multiple studies have shown that working more than fifty-five hours proportionately diminishes productivity. More recent research shows that thirty-two hours might be optimal. With the right team members, you can and should work less to do more. God knew this in the beginning, when he set the rhythm.

Dennis Prager, in *The Rational Bible, Exodus*, reveals that being required to take a day off elevates us from a slave mentality to those who are sovereign and choose their lifestyle. In the Christian faith, we are sons and daughters of the Most High God. We have free will. We were bought with a price to worship Jesus, and that comes with privileges. Rest is guaranteed and required. No other false god gave this edict.

Prager points out that with no work on Shabbat, or your day of rest, we naturally look for ways to be with others. Communities grow stronger when they spend time together, first with immediate family, then local community, and beyond. This gives us, in the Judeo-Christian world, immense strength in times of peril.

Social media and TV have reduced the tendency to connect, the negative effects of which are now widely known. Disengaging from the process of meeting your needs—think perpetual farming, hunting, and gathering—allows for greater creativity and an increased *desire* to work. To keep a day holy is to acknowledge the Creator. Prager teaches that seven-day weeks do not coincide with any cosmological rhythm, either. Anyone who has spent time processing payroll knows that there are 4.3 weeks in a month—not exactly a round number! God decided the roles of the natural world, then established the week at the end of creation. Reference Genesis:

> Then God said, "Let lights appear in the sky to separate the day from the night. Let them be signs to mark the seasons, days, and years. Let these lights in the sky shine down on the earth." And that is what happened. God made two great lights—the larger one to govern the day, and the smaller one to govern the night. He also made the stars. God set these lights in the sky to light the earth, to govern the day and night, and to separate the light from the darkness. And God saw that it was good. And evening passed and morning came, marking the fourth day." (Gen. 1:14-19)

The Shabbat is a supernatural timing system. The Most High God is the only supernatural being to require this. Overlay this with the fact that no animal on planet earth rests on any particular day—proof positive for creation rather than evolution.

Before we wrap up establishing a properly prioritized personal and professional relationship with Jesus, there is one more from the first half of His ten statements or guidelines for life. This is the piece that often creates the tallest barrier in the way of a complete relationship with God. Honor your parents. Not to worry, He saw this coming as well.

The Boardroom or Bible Study

For group discussion and individual journaling:

When has the power of your words produced tremendous fruit? Caused immense damage?

What will you do to increase fruit and reduce damage?

When is the best time for you to rest? How do you ensure that you get enough? If not, what will you change?

CHAPTER 10

THE BIG TEN FOR BUSINESS: VERTICAL ALIGNMENT

> "My heroes are and were my parents. I can't see having anyone else as my heroes."
> –Michael Jordan

Vertical alignment is the skeleton, or backbone, of your faith. Stability rooted in God's word, with your eyes constantly on Him makes you unshakeable, like Him. Generational curses are spiritual, psychological, and even genetic, but they can be overcome. Before God teaches us how to interact with others, He addresses the source of the most deeply embedded challenges humans face, our parents. This command precedes His call not to commit murder.

God's fifth value statement—fifth rule for life—is equally important to business but might not be as obvious. The fifth commandment or statement reads:

> Honor your father and your mother, that your days may be long in the land that the Lord your God is giving you. (Exod. 20:12 ESV)

Right now, I'd be asking, "Jerry, this is certainly important, but what does it have to do with business?"

The pinnacle of business is leadership. The first leaders assigned to you—by God—are your parents. By requiring honor to those appointed above us, we learn to respect authority (Prager, 2022). As you know, we will have good bosses and bad bosses, great clients and less than desirable ones. Learning to control ourselves when we don't get our way starts with parents.

Whether you had great parents, mediocre parents, or the worst ever born, you did not choose them. Honoring your father and your mother is showing honor to God.

How?

He picked them. There is an absolute beautiful passage of scripture that details how He did this:

> You made all the delicate, inner parts of my body and knit me together in my mother's womb.
> Thank you for making me so wonderfully complex! Your workmanship is marvelous—how well I know it.
> You watched me as I was being formed in utter seclusion, as I was woven together in the dark of the womb.
> You saw me before I was born.
> Every day of my life was recorded in your book.
> Every moment was laid out before a single day had passed.
> How precious are your thoughts about me, O God.
> They cannot be numbered!
> I can't even count them; they outnumber the grains of sand! And when I wake up, you are still with me! (Ps. 139:13-18, emphasis added)

I still get tears when I meditate on this. Look closely how the psalmist reveals God's appreciation for everything about us and that He loved us before a single day had passed.

Before Genesis, He knew you. Before "Light Be!" or Adam's fall or David's anointing, you were precious to Him.

> **Before Genesis, He knew you, before "Light Be!" or Adam's fall or David's anointing, you were precious to Him**

To honor one's father and mother, no matter how terrible they were to you, is to truly believe that God wanted them to be a part of your life here on earth. Although *without* sin, to be *made* sin, and all of God's wrath for humanity toward sin emptied upon Him, no one has suffered worse than the Lord Jesus. Isaiah describes it well:

> He was despised and rejected—a man of sorrows, acquainted with deepest grief. We turned our backs on him and looked the other way. He was despised, and we did not care. Yet it was our weaknesses he carried; it was our sorrows that weighed him down. And we thought his troubles were a punishment from God, a punishment for his own sins! But he was pierced for our rebellion, crushed for our sins. He was beaten so we could be whole. He was whipped so we could be healed. All of us, like sheep, have strayed away. We have left God's paths to follow our own. Yet the Lord laid on him the sins of us all. (Isa. 53:3-6)

Even as parents ourselves, we can never know what torment our father and mother experienced. There is a chance that you dislike them for a misinterpreted memory. Imperfect like us, they may have strayed from God's perfect will.

Both Paul in the third chapter of his letter to the Romans, versus ten through twelve and the Psalmist remind us, "But no, all have turned away; all have become corrupt. No one does good, not a single one!" (Ps. 14:3).

Do you trust God? Can you?

Jesus forgave those who sent him to die the worst death known to man. By forgiving your parents, and honoring them (I didn't say love them, we'll get to that), you are releasing your soul from the bondage they created. If you were a victim of kidnapping, abuse of any kind, bullying due to decisions your parents made, now is the time to give that to Jesus. Here's how Peter teaches us to do that:

> So humble yourselves under the mighty power of God, and *at the right time he will lift you up in honor*. Give all your worries and cares to God, for he cares about you. Stay alert! Watch out for your great enemy, the devil. He prowls around like a roaring lion, looking for someone to devour. Stand firm against him, and be strong in your faith. Remember that your family of *believers all over the world* is going through the same kind of suffering you are. (1 Pet. 5:6-9, emphasis added)

The strength that you gained through a terrible experience is a gift from God. The mess of your life is your ministry. Those suffering the way you did will benefit from your story. Tell it.

Think of it as your *Failure Resumé*. Like a corporate resumé, we can list periods of time in our lives full of events and actions about which we are ashamed. Whether you did it or it was done to you, God's strength is perfectly revealed in our weakness. Sharing weakness reveals to the world God's work in you!

Please note also that "honoring your father and your mother" was distinctively written with individual possession by God to indicate equality (Prager, 2022). Just as we were created male and female in God's image, we are to honor both parents equally. This is emphasized later in Leviticus as mother is written first:

> Each of you must show great respect for your mother and father, and you must always observe my Sabbath days of rest. I am the Lord your God. (Lev. 19:3, emphasis added)

Let's now address honor versus love. It does not say, love your mother and your father. God understands that this may be impossible for you on this side of the grave. To honor them is to treat them with respect behind their backs and face to face. It is very much okay if you have to keep them more than arm's length away to keep your sanity.

> **HONOR DAD AND MOM: HONOR THE PAST**

God's fifth rule for a quality life can be remembered as, HONOR DAD AND MOM. In business we would say, HONOR THE PAST. None of us got anywhere alone. There were parents, guardians, teachers, coaches, professors, and friends that we can credit with helping us.

Society today, marveling at its own brilliance, has rejected long held wisdom. Judgment of yesterday by today's standards is the norm. It seems we are insistent on reinventing the proverbial wheel.

It's also the first command with a reward. This indicates an impact on posterity, beyond your earthly existence. To live long in the land essentially means your children will continue to possess the land God has given you. Translated to today, honoring your father and mother teaches your children to do the same. They won't have to start from the bottom and can build on your efforts (Prager, 2022). Solomon writes in Proverbs:

> Good people leave an inheritance to their grandchildren, but the sinner's wealth passes to the godly. (Prov. 13:22)

Teaching children to honor you starts with observed behavior. "Do as I say, not as I do," is not godly in the least. Paul details to the church at Philippi both how Jesus honored His Father and set an example for us:

> You must have the same attitude that Christ Jesus had. Though he was God, he did not think of equality with God as something to cling to. Instead, he gave up his divine privileges; he took the humble position of a slave and was born as a human being. When he appeared in human form, he humbled himself in obedience to God and died a criminal's death on a cross. Therefore, God elevated him to the place of highest honor and gave him the name above all other names, that at the name of Jesus every knee should bow, in heaven and on earth and under the earth, and every tongue declare that Jesus Christ is Lord, to the glory of God the Father. (Phil. 2:5-11)

God has a place of immense honor for you, and you need to get your children off on the right foot. They may stray but will ultimately return to Him if you set the example. Jesus elevates His fifth commandment in Matthew's gospel:

> Jesus replied, "And why do you break the command of God for the sake of your tradition? For God said, 'Honor your father and mother' and 'Anyone who curses their father or mother is to be put to death.' But you say that if anyone declares that what might have been used to help their father or mother is 'devoted to God,' They are not to 'honor their father or mother' with it. Thus you nullify the word of God for the sake of your tradition. (Matt. 15:3–6, NIV)

Paul writes to the church at Ephesus with a twist for Dads:

> Children, obey your parents because you belong to the Lord, for this is the right thing to do. "Honor your father and mother." This is the first commandment with a promise: If you honor your father and mother, "things will go well for you, and you will have a long life on the earth." Fathers, do not provoke your children to anger by the way you treat them. Rather, bring them up with the discipline and instruction that comes from the Lord. (Eph. 6:1-4)

The emphasis is on things going well in life as a reward. Why?

> **Every business is established on a foundational principle, that principle is the parent of the organization**

Parents have the first and biggest influence on how children will act into adulthood. By age four, most of this groundwork has been laid. By eight, morals have been established. If gone wrong, only a heart transplant from the Lord can correct those issues. And it might not be our parents' fault!

Encouraging words from a loving father have considerable power. Dads, your words resonate in perpetuity for your children's lives. Don't waste them.

Every business is established on a foundational principle. This principle, or ideal, is the parent of the business. Valuing your parents entails recognizing their values and rules and respecting them. In business, we recognize the values of the company and respect them. The same applies to respecting mentors and authorities.

The US military is struggling to recruit, and those who are recruited cannot meet minimum entry level physical fitness requirements. This can be directly tied to our influence—or lack thereof—in our children in the last forty years.

Here's a hard truth many will not like. Video games, man caves, and male bashing TV shows, portraying blundering-idiot-father cartoons as well as sitcoms, perpetuate a false narrative. Video games can be a great escape, and I love when my kids play them while driving to vacation spots—a car never gets so quiet! They are an immense time suck. I've played plenty and never realized how much time passed until I finally broke free. For many, it changes brain chemistry, particularly in young people.

Despite the argument for hand-eye coordination, it does not prepare you to throw or kick a ball. Dr. Andy Royalty, founder and owner of *The Royal Treatment* physical therapy and gold performance company, says, "In fitness, motion is lotion." for the joints. Sitting in front of a massive digital screen for eight hours is bad for you.

Admittedly, my home office could be considered a "man cave." The difference is, I use the space to contribute to the kingdom of God. I meet with and teach my children here. In most cases, the door is open, and they can enter at any time, or play on the floor if they want.

If you have a "man cave" or "she shed," is the door open? What happens when it is closed? Connection with family is your number one priority. Don't hide.

Since the shows, *Rosanne* and *The Simpsons*, boys and girls from the '90s and beyond have grown up watching these worthless father figures on TV. There was a show on HBO, called *Louie*, that topped the chart for worst father portrayal. I'd take Tony Soprano over him. I like how the mothers are often portrayed as strong and intelligent, but good men, Christian or otherwise, cannot be so weak!

Women who are with a strong, reliable, intelligent man are not sad about that. Be one and reap the rewards.

Dad and mom, be respectable. Teach them to honor you. Go throw the football, softball, or baseball with your sons and daughters. Build a pillow fort or read a book together if you prefer indoor activities. Turn off the digital devices. Make it a requirement, and suffer through the initial complaining. They will get on board fast and eventually look forward to it.

Talk to them every day—if only for a few minutes. Let them tell you the most exciting thing that happened and the worst thing. Ask them hard questions about life, starting as young as possible. Make a routine—mine is "piggyback rides to the third floor," or "hugs on my back" as we lay in bed. I used to read to them and tickle them while saying good night. It takes less than ten minutes per day and is more meaningful than a week at a theme park.

Believe it or not, they worship you. They want you. They cannot get enough of you, no matter how screwed up you are!

Need a nudge?

How's this—when my oldest two children were two and just turning one, I spent my twenty-eighth birthday, not with them, but in jail for a bench warrant from an unpaid court fee. The charge: drunk in public. For my thirtieth birthday, when they were two years older, I was in jail for two convictions of driving under the influence inside twelve months! Straight time is no joke, but it didn't even make an impact on them.

How?

I cleaned up, followed God, and taught them how to do the same. Today, and for many years, they have watched me in the pursuit of God, family, and our dreams. Stumble I may as a parent, but by His grace and some intentionality, they are both amazing student athletes and are now in college. Praise God, I have two more coming right along with a similar trajectory.

Today, I frequently have what I call, "meaningful dialogue" with all of my children. If you are not sure what that means, just wait until your children are teenagers, then you will long desperately for one of two types of conversations: simple, childlike stream-of-consciousness, listening or meaningful dialogue!

Here's some encouragement. My oldest and I fought daily about curfew, phones, and anything else for most of her high school experience. Despite that, toward the end of her sophomore year in college, she told me someone asked her, "who was the most influential person in your life so far." She said whether she liked it or not, she couldn't conclude anyone other than me!

> **God only needs a mustard seed of faith and a broken piece of clay to perform miracles**

Can you believe that?

Jailbird Jerry, influential. God only needs a mustard seed of faith and a broken piece of clay to perform miracles. Fathers, even the fights have meaning. Don't give up in high school and beyond—lean in more. This is when they need you the most. They don't know how important the decisions they make are, but you do! You are fighting for their future, just as Jesus fought for ours!

So far we've learned five policies, or decision-making guides, from God's value statements. These protect our soul gates, or senses: the mind, will, and emotions. Figure 3 lists our vertical alignment steps, translated as: Jesus is CEO, Follow Truth, Words Have Power, Praise-Perform-Pray and Honor the Past, as foundation for our the proper attitude. Next is our actions and horizontal alignment!

Figure 3

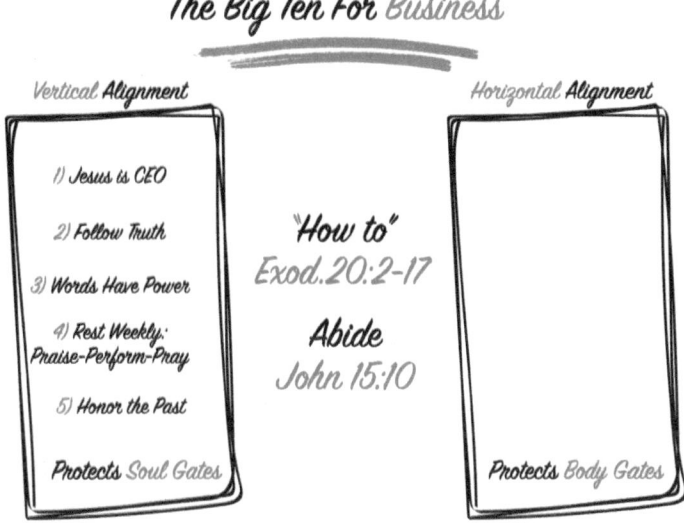

Note. Our soul needs daily alignment grounded in Jesus as CEO.

The Boardroom or Bible Study

For group discussion and individual journaling:

Do you believe the pain and suffering in your life has meaning? Why or why not?

When have you seen the thread of God's hand through the tapestry of your life?

What are two things that your parents deserve honor for?

Name three people who helped you get to another level in life? What did they contribute?

What is the parental principle of your family? Team? Organization?

What miracles have you seen in your life?

What mustard seed of faith and broken jar of clay have you given God?

CHAPTER 11

THE BIG TEN FOR BUSINESS: PLAYING WELL WITH OTHERS

> "A leader is one who knows the way, goes the way, and shows the way."
> —John C. Maxwell

While vertical alignment is the foundation, God's purpose for you before the return of his Son, our Lord Jesus, is one hundred percent about playing well with others. Recall the Great Commission:

> Therefore, go and make disciples of all the nations, baptizing them in the name of the Father and the Son and the Holy Spirit. Teach these new disciples to obey all the commands I have given you... (Matt. 28:19–20a)

We are called to multiply ourselves.

How?

Make a friend, introduce them to Jesus, and teach them His ways of overcoming challenges.

Simple, right?

At *Jerry Howard International*, we make content through video, writing and speaking that equips leaders for this mission. Our team of specialists, *iNTREPiD iMPACT Team*, engages with business owners and company executives to teach leaders how to deploy these resources into their lives, families and organizations at scale. Ideally, leaders multiply themselves within organizations, just as we are in the agency, following the example of Jesus.

It's worth noting that although Jesus didn't call it "the great commission," we know that any directive coming from Him is great! Even the word co-mission implies the involvement of others. This brings us to God's sixth guideline for an amazing, abundant and awesome existence, despite our fallen world:

> You must not murder. (Exod. 20:13)

At first glance it seems pretty obvious.

You cannot teach anyone anything if you end their life. If we restate this as an actionable phrase, it's simply: RESPECT HUMAN LIFE. We were all created in the image of God, the *Imago Dei*, as stated in Latin. That covers all humans. However, when we are reborn in spirit as a Christian, we now must walk as Christ bearers. We are now bearers of the anointing Jesus carried. He walked in pure love.

If we bear the pain and suffering of slugging through Leviticus (just kidding!), then we read where God gives more specificity to His initial command:

> **RESPECT HUMAN LIFE**

> Do not *nurse hatred in your heart* for any of your relatives. Confront people directly so you will not be held guilty for their sin. Do not seek revenge or bear a grudge against a fellow Israelite, but love your neighbor as yourself. I am the LORD. (Lev. 19:17–18, emphasis added)

Remember, Jesus elevated the moral laws. Since Leviticus gave an adequate picture of this being a *heart* issue, Jesus didn't need to elevate this per se, but merely reinforce and give more context:

> You have heard that our ancestors were told, 'You must not murder. If you commit murder, you are subject to judgment.' But I say, if you are even angry with someone, you are subject to judgment! If you call someone an idiot, you are in danger of being brought before the court. And if you curse someone, you are in danger of the fires of hell. (Matt. 5:21–22)

Jesus goes on to detail just how important this was:

> So if you are presenting a sacrifice at the altar in the Temple and you suddenly remember that someone has something against you, leave your sacrifice there at the altar. Go and be reconciled to that person. Then come and offer your sacrifice to God. (Matt. 5:23–24)

> **Before you offer anything to God, love your enemy**

Before you offer anything to God, love others. God doesn't need your money or your donations. Giving is a joy that teaches you basic fiscal responsibility. He does need your obedience to Jesus so you can live your best life. He wants you to help get His people into the kingdom of heaven. If you continually hold grudges with everyone, very soon no one will want your company. More importantly, *you* won't want anyone's company. I speak from experience when I say grudges produce an extreme cynicism toward people in general.

My personality is one of three primary gifts: leadership, encouragement, and teaching. This comes with a high level of empathy. Empathy is great, until it's not. Those with a high sensitivity to other's emotions are also equally susceptible to the negative effects of those same interactions. Simply put, I feel deeply.

Not only that, but I am also predisposed to the classical Jungian characterization of introvert. My definition is, one who tends to hold back outward presentation until a certain comfort level exists in a situation. Holding back allows negativity to build up and results in unresolved anger. Later, at some unsuspecting moment, it explodes outward! An emotional Tasmanian devil unleashes on those closest to me. My wife calls it, "drunk on anger."

Two things mitigate this build up. First, I need to know my value to Jesus. As His little brother for whom He died, and an heir to God's kingdom with a specific purpose, I am shielded from the downward spiral of negative self-talk and the lie that I'm not valued by others. This knowledge can only come by spending time in His word and in prayer. Second, I have learned to communicate with others from a place of optimistic curiosity as to their position on any given topic.

Can you imagine how many problems could get solved on the world stage if global leaders took these two actions?

I know you can. Leaders in business are where the rubber meets the road. We define the culture through our attitude and actions, not the six or eight words, often called mission statement, on the wall of the lobby or conference room. If our actions and attitudes are consistent with the "plaque on the wall," then they have meaning. It begins with us.

Recall how many times you've ignored your own values with your family, friends, and colleagues. For me, I cannot count that high. Peter, just like all of us, tried hard to find the loophole when he asked how many times he had to forgive someone if they sinned against Him:

> Then Peter came to him and asked, "Lord, how often should I forgive someone who sins against me? Seven times?" "No, not seven times," Jesus replied, "but seventy times seven!" (Matt. 18:21–22)

Jesus' point was you either walk in love or you don't. There's no limit to God's love. Thus, there can be no limit to ours.

How many vendors, bad customers, dishonest employees have you "given a piece of your mind?"

To lash out at them is to step into the very bait that Satan laid for you. In essence, you really do go momentarily insane and give them a piece of your sanity.

> **Giving a "piece of your mind" is a literal action**

Ultimately, your reputation and business suffer, not the recipient of your outrage. But to handle yourself with maturity is Godlike. Paul quotes Proverbs when he teaches:

> Dear friends, never take revenge. Leave that to the righteous anger of God. For the Scriptures say, "I will take revenge; I will pay them back," says the LORD. Instead, "If your enemies are hungry, feed them. If they are thirsty, give them something to drink. In doing this, you will heap burning coals of shame on their heads." Don't let evil conquer you, but conquer evil by doing good. (Rom. 12:19–21)

How much time and money, both taxpayer money and private wealth, has been spent on attacking another out of anger?

With the number of lawsuits today, I love Jesus' final teaching on anger:

> When you are on the way to court with your adversary, settle your differences quickly. Otherwise, your accuser may hand you over to the judge, who will hand you over to an officer, and you will be thrown into prison. And if that happens, you surely won't be free again until you have paid the last penny. (Matt. 5:25–26)

Prison!?

As a business person who has taken many risks, not all of which have worked out for me and my partners, I'm certainly glad it doesn't typically come to that in the west.

Prison of the heart though, is a real thing. Unforgiveness is a prison for you, not the target of your anger. Only you can unlock the door.

Here's a technique I find fun. Say to yourself, "[insert person's name] is no longer my enemy, my mental ninjas will not attack them and slice them into tiny little bits and pieces of carcass to be devoured by vultures along the side of the road. They are now perfectly safe to walk the streets of my mind." Tell me that doesn't make you smile just a bit at the thought of your *former* enemy!

All fun aside, as a Christ bearer, and a leader in business, you are required to walk in love. Your position is a gift from God, and you need to steward it appropriately. Furthermore, you can be angry and not sin. You can also be angry at God and not sin. His love for us is infinite, He can handle anything you throw at him. By being angry at Him, you are acknowledging both Him and His control over the situation. I say, be angry! Get it all out! Then walk in love, for Him and the people around you. The Apostle John's first letter states:

> Anyone who hates another brother or sister is really a murderer at heart. And you know that murderers don't have eternal life within them. We know what real love is because Jesus gave up his life for us. So we

also ought to give up our lives for our brothers and sisters. If someone has enough money to live well and sees a brother or sister in need but shows no compassion—how can God's love be in that person? (1 John 3:15–17)

To give up your life is more than just dying for our faith. It is subordinating your mind, will, and emotions to the teaching of Jesus Christ. The proverbial death is of your *ego*.

From the Garden to the present, mankind has insisted on getting its way. If you are going to walk as a Christ bearer, then let's go all in! If so, we need to remember what Paul teaches about the potter and the clay:

> Well then, you might say, "Why does God blame people for not responding? Haven't they simply done what he makes them do?" No, don't say that. Who are you, a mere human being, to argue with God? Should the thing that was created say to the one who created it, "Why have you made me like this?" When a potter makes jars out of clay, doesn't he have a right to use the same lump of clay to make one jar for decoration and another to throw garbage into? In the same way, even though God has the right to show his anger and his power, he is very patient with those on whom his anger falls, who are destined for destruction. He does this to make the riches of his glory shine even brighter on those to whom he shows mercy, who were prepared in advance for glory. And we are among those whom he selected, both from the Jews and from the Gentiles. (Rom 9:19–24)

In business, it should go without saying that murder is wrong.

Have we considered what businesses, intentionally or otherwise, do harm? How does your business or employer impact the community? Do you support businesses that have questionable practices? When investing, with whom are you pooling your money?

Even donor directed funds may be contributing to adolescent transgender treatment; which you know I strongly oppose. Personally, I'm still trying to find a way to disconnect from things made in China. The point is, do not murder means far more than not killing your neighbor. Remember, honor human life.

The Boardroom or Bible Study

For group discussion and individual journaling:

Why does God want you to love your enemy before you make any sacrifice to Him?

How did Jesus elevate the do not murder law to respect human life? How do you live that out with your enemies?

When have you gone momentarily insane giving someone a piece of your mind? Did the situation improve? Worsen? How?

How did you reconcile? If not, can you? What will you do? If not, what is the one thing you can always do?

CHAPTER 12

THE BIG TEN FOR BUSINESS: YOUR MOST IMPORTANT CONTRACT

> "The law is about you looking at yourself. The New Covenant is all about you seeing Jesus."
> –Joseph Prince

The strongest unit in the western world is family. As far back as history has been recorded, it was known to be true. Until recently, family was considered a good arrangement for men, primarily for posterity, and for women and children for security and protection, respectively. Over time, it was assumed that certain roles were best, even when they weren't.

About a hundred years ago, science began questioning the validity of long held institutions such as marriage and family. As usual, the experts were wrong, marriage really is good. Roles such as homemaker, in the last fifty years viewed as oppressive to women, are reemerging as one of honor for men and women alike. As someone who was a stay-at-home dad of two small children, then later when between careers, I cared for an infant, a toddler, and two in elementary school, I can personally speak to its challenges and rewards.

Recently, there has been an increasing amount of work published to reinforce the belief that marriage is good. Steven Nock from University of Virginia, summarizes Scott Loveless and his colleagues from *The Family in the New Millennium*, by writing:

> They make the case for the proposition that marriage is an important public health and safety issue. It is a legitimate concern of all governments, and they should make every effort to promote and protect it. But they should do more than encourage it. Marriage should be privileged in law and public policy. Married people are doing something for their societies when they care for their families, provide for, protect, and control their children. They are doing something by protecting their health. They are doing something by maintaining stable and orderly lives. If they were not doing all these things, then their governments would have to, and their nations would be weakened. (2007)

Dr. Jordan Peterson, a widely popular, leading clinical psychologist, asserts that men in particular need companionship and a purpose directly in front of them. On Biblical theory, I do not agree with him, particularly because his assertions are lacking the factual perspective of the documented supernatural. However, I emphatically celebrate his desire to understand God's word and lead others to pursue the same. With the Holy Spirit, we can all enjoy the amplified synergy that comes with it!

Obviously, I have a Biblical worldview. But psychologically, Dr. Peterson nails it when teaching men to "make something of themselves, particularly with family" (2023).

Not much was known about the psychological benefits of marriage until society began to question its importance. Peterson, much to my joy, emphasizes this consistently. We've witnessed the breakdown of many facets of a good working society since marriage abandonment became the norm. This ancient institution's primary benefits are trust and accountability. Women, particularly those with children, typically develop this to some degree, naturally, but not men. Marriage does great things for men, and he not only believes, but teaches and practices this!

My friend and the founding pastor of our church, Hope Point Church in Chesterfield, VA, Dr. Steve Stells, co-authored a book called *Perfect Design*. As a retired senior pastor, he is also a business owner and consultant to other transitioning pastors. His consultancy and the book detail the importance of healthy succession planning and its execution inside the church. Steve states, "Money is the medium of exchange in this world, but in the kingdom of heaven it's trust."

> **We've witnessed the breakdown of many facets of a good working society since marriage abandonment became the norm**

The foundation of any family both in eastern and western cultures, no matter how far back you look, is marriage. The foundation of marriage is unequivocally, trust. God's seventh guiding principle for a great life is written this way:

You must not commit adultery. (Exod. 20:14)

The unsaved might offer the question, "Why not?" or, "What does this have to do with business?"

Trust.

Traditional marriage, that between a man and a woman, before witnesses and God, is more than a contract, it's a covenant. The difference being that contracts are social and societal, therefore, can be altered or abolished. A covenant is spiritual; it cannot be changed or revoked. God does not change. Consequently, any arrangement He sanctions cannot be changed.

Adultery is an act against your spouse, your family (and its future), and against God. Those who do not believe in God can still use logic to discover the importance of trust and accountability to preserving family. Since we are believers in God and followers of the way of Jesus, we need to honor this. Jesus reinforced it spiritually as well:

> But Jesus responded, "He wrote this commandment [referring to divorce] only as a concession to your hard hearts. But 'God made them male and female' from the beginning of creation. 'This explains why a man leaves his father and mother and is joined to his wife, the two are united into one.' Since they are no longer two but one, *let no one split apart what God has joined together.*" (Mark 10:5-9, emphasis added)

But it's just sex, right?

Sexual intercourse is spiritual. Ever wondered why rape is so much worse than assault?

It's spiritual.

At the time of creation, God took woman from man so that he would not be alone. Thus, to rejoin with one another is a return to origin, of sorts. The covenant is between a man, a woman, and God. This triune relationship of three parts, all independent and simultaneously intradependent, is the earthly representation of Father, Son, and Holy Spirit.

I know God is the Father, but whether it's man or woman who represents the Holy Spirit, I'm not certain. I would say my wife has the most spirit, particularly when I screw up, but it's not always holy!

Seriously, though, most times when we fight it's because she's so incredible to me.

Then why do we fight?

My repeated mistake is rooted in holding her to some impossible standard. When she doesn't meet it, I get disrespectful. She doesn't take disrespect lightly, nor should she!

Technically, when a man and woman join intimately, the body, mind and spirit are activated in ways that no other action can produce. Specific details on the science behind this are beyond the scope of this book, but I encourage you to run a few quick searches on the subject. Jesus definitely elevated this command when he said:

> You have heard the commandment that says, 'You must not commit adultery.' But I say, anyone *who even looks at a woman with lust has already committed adultery* with her in his heart. So if your eye—even your good eye—causes you to lust, gouge it out and throw it away. It is better for you to lose one part of your body than for your whole body to be thrown into hell. And if your hand—even your stronger hand—causes you to sin, cut it off and throw it away. It is better for you to lose one part of your body than for your whole body to be thrown into hell. (Matt. 5:27–30, emphasis added)

Even looking at another woman? Or man?

Yes. I'm certain this applies to women lusting for those other than their spouse as well.

Why?

Jesus knows our heart is the guiding force to our actions. Before I go further, as a disciple of Jesus, you have been forgiven and justified from all sin. Hold that close in case you are freaking out about that movie you watched last night or that post on social media you stared at too long. Your job is to break those habits, and I will cover that later in this chapter. I just want you to know Jesus' standard on the subject!

We know marriage is good. We know adultery is bad. What about business?

Contracts exist to hold one person accountable to another, but they are broken all the time.

How do people feel when that occurs?

When you honor your spouse, you honor your children, your family, and your reputation.

If marriage is good and it is literally the backbone of family, then it should be the one contract that could never be defiled, at least in your mind.

How healthy or reliable is a person at work when he or she is causing their marriage to fail? When someone spends all of their time trying to deceive their spouse, how accountable is that person to the work they were hired to do?

Simply put, and brace yourself because this is a hard teaching, they are overcome with lust and are not trustworthy.

Only through repentance, and a long-term period of time through which trust with others is not broken, can someone be considered honorable again. This is a tough fact, I know.

What if the couple reconciles?

That's great! But depending on who violated the covenant, they will be majorly suspect for a long time. Every time the offending party goes somewhere alone, the spouse is wondering. Trust can be rebuilt, but not without challenge. God's grace is sufficient, so my prayer is that all marriages are restored, but we are human, and suspicious, and broken. It takes time.

> **CHERISH YOUR SPOUSE: HONOR AGREEMENTS**

If we remove the "not" and create an actionable phrase, CHERISH YOUR SPOUSE is easy enough to remember. In business, we might say: HONOR AGREEMENTS. This applies to your private and thought life as well. I know, and I'm still working at this, it requires immense persistence!

Please note, as someone reborn in Christ, filled with the Holy Spirit, you cannot be possessed by demons, but your adversary has eons of practice manipulating humans. Whispers, old memories, and circumstances can be manipulated to entice you to sin. Replace your thoughts with God's. Controlling your thoughts and knowing that not all of what you think is from you are the first steps to controlling your actions. Controlling your actions will keep you on the true and honorable path.

It's the same in business.

When you get off track and don't pay an employee according to the terms agreed upon hire, how long before they quit? If you break a contract, how long before you get more opportunities? Or worse, how long before you are in court?

It's the same with paying off debt. If you file bankruptcy, you have some protection, but you are subject to the consequences.

It is worth noting that the bankruptcy laws in the US were set up to encourage risk in business. This does contribute to economic growth, and I believe is a hallmark of its prosperity. It is proven that if you do your due diligence and work hard, you can succeed in small business and grow beyond.

It is good for entrepreneurs to create jobs and contribute to the GDP if they are able. There remain many variables out of one's control, so the risk is high. Faith in God and execution of His Big Ten will certainly shift the odds in your favor! And there is nothing wrong with being a reliable employee. As an executive and business owner multiple times over, I know good people are hard to find!

God's calling may be in the business you start, buy, or work in—or in the failure of it.

Even if it shuts down?

Yes. I learned quite a bit about leadership when one of our businesses had to be closed after the Covid lockdowns. Here's what Paul writes to the Romans about adversity:

> And the Holy Spirit helps us in our weakness. For example, we don't know what God wants us to pray for. But the Holy Spirit prays for us with groanings that cannot be expressed in words. And the Father who knows all hearts knows what the Spirit is saying, for the Spirit pleads for us believers in harmony with God's own will. And we know that *God causes everything to work together for the good of those who love God and are called according to his purpose for them.* (Rom. 8:26–28, emphasis added)

Although God calls everything to work together for the good, not everything is good. This scripture, often taken out of context and misused, is about prayer and faith. We can't see or know God's full plan. We must trust Him.

For those of us who are called, that is followers of Jesus, our faith in Him through the challenges ultimately brings good to us. We must persevere. More specifically, the decaying fruit of the curse—poverty, disease, despair—are not God's plan for you. Yet, we live in a fallen world, so remaining steadfast despite those outcomes will produce good fruit in your life.

In Psalm 13, David illustrates this mental transition beautifully. First, he cries out like any normal, rational human going through hard times. Then, in Verse five, by changing his words, he shifts his thoughts to that of one with faith in God. He concludes in verse six with action to push through the misery. Singing in worship to the Lord for His goodness. He writes:

> O Lord, how long will you forget me? Forever?
> How long will you look the other way?
> How long must I struggle with anguish in my soul,
> with sorrow in my heart every day?
> How long will my enemy have the upper hand?
> Turn and answer me, O Lord my God!
> Restore the sparkle to my eyes, or I will die.
> Don't let my enemies gloat, saying, "We have defeated him!"
> Don't let them rejoice at my downfall.
> But I trust in your unfailing love.
> I will rejoice because you have rescued me.
> I will sing to the Lord
> because he is good to me. (Ps. 13:1–6)

To the church at Philippi, Paul details the same process, revealing what I call a New Testament perspective on how this is accomplished and the corresponding fruit:

> Don't worry about anything; instead, pray about everything. Tell God what you need, and thank him for all he has done. Then you will experience God's peace, which exceeds anything we can understand. His peace will guard your hearts and minds as you live in Christ Jesus. (Phil. 4:6–7)

By walking in God's purpose, we have all that we need to fulfill His resolve. Circumstances do not dictate success, and worry is not necessary. In business, when you honor your agreements, at the most basic level, you are walking in commitment.

Following the Big Ten will cause God's specific, perfectly designed, one-of-a-kind plan for your life to light up like the yellow brick road right in front of you. David's Psalm gives great credence to this position. Read slowly because each line is equally worth meditation on its own. Verse 105, the first verse below, illuminates it best, and we know that David was "a man after [God's] own heart" (1 Sam 13:14). The rest of these verses detail his commitment to God's guidance for a great life:

> Your word is a lamp to guide my feet and a light for my path.
> I've promised it once, and I'll promise it again:
> I will obey your righteous regulations.
> I have suffered much, O LORD;
> restore my life again as you promised.
> LORD, accept my offering of praise,
> and teach me your regulations.
> My life constantly hangs in the balance,
> but I will not stop obeying your instructions.
> The wicked have set their traps for me,
> but I will not turn from your commandments.
> Your laws are my treasure;
> they are my heart's delight.
> I am determined to keep your decrees
> to the very end. (Ps. 119:105–112)

Your covenant with God, through the cross, is the most important agreement you have in body, soul, and spirit, in this life and eternity. Second only to that is your marriage. Remember, your work in this life is preparation for the next. There is a reward both now and in heaven. Do your best.

As a follower of the way of Jesus, your soul is the true battleground. Jesus won your spirit, and you have been reborn. All sin, past and future has been wiped from God's memory. This is called justification by faith. Consequently, your mind, will, and emotions need to be sanctified. That takes time but can be done. Again, Paul, the greatest evangelist and teacher to the Gentiles, details this in his letter to the Romans. Here's how it works:

> And so, dear brothers and sisters, I plead with you to give your bodies to God because of all he has done for you. Let them be a living and holy sacrifice—the kind he will find acceptable. This is truly the way to worship him. Don't copy the behavior and customs of this world, but let God transform you into a new person by changing the way you think. Then you will learn to know God's will for you, which is good and pleasing and perfect. (Rom 12:1–2)

I've found the easiest way to resist lustful thoughts is to give them to God. When I find myself gazing too long at a member of the opposite sex, I simply look away. Next, I take a moment to recognize that habit was from my life before Jesus. You might imagine laying that lustful habit at the foot of the throne room of Grace every time you correct yourself. Soon enough, it stays at the foot of the cross.

Does this sound too ethereal?

"Take captive every thought to make it obedient to Christ," is exactly what Paul, in his second letter, told the church at Corinth (2 Cor. 10:5, NIV).

Science has finally caught up to give proof of Romans 12:2 to the skeptics! Look up Warren Lamb. Not unlike most of us Marines before Boot Camp, he was a self-professed tough guy growing up, then a US Marine Scout Sniper in Vietnam, then became a clinical psychologist. After converting to Christ at thirty-one, he has spent the last thirty-five years studying how to rewire the brain for high-end trauma patients (kidnapping and human trafficking victims). He has verified through FMRI testing, using ONLY God's word, no surgery, no pharmacology, no psychedelics, that neuro pathways can be altered. You can physically and literally change your mind! (Lamb, 2024).

Neuroplasticity is a relatively new field that confirms Lamb's studies. Of course, God the Creator knew all along. He inspired Paul to write extensively about it to the Romans and Philippians. The verse bears repeating:

> "Do not be conformed to this world, but be transformed by the renewal of your mind." (Rom 12:2, ESV)

> Be anxious for nothing, but in everything by prayer and supplication, with thanksgiving, let your requests be made known to God. (Phil. 4:6, NKJV)

> Fix your thoughts on what is true, and honorable, and right, and pure, and lovely, and admirable. Think about things that are excellent and worthy of praise. (Phil. 4:8, NLT)

To be honest, I can't say that I avoid all movies that have intimate scenes, but how I handle that is the key. Fast-forward or look away. The absolute best rule of thumb is asking, "Would I watch this with one of my daughters at the age of eleven?" If the answer is no, it's time to change that habit! Remember, Paul says not to copy the behaviors and customs of this world, and everywhere you look, you are still in this world. It's not easy; it takes practice and persistence.

In my heart, I don't believe any of us truly wants easy. You never know how strong you are until you conquer something hard. David didn't fight Goliath right away. First, he was anointed, then filled with the Holy Spirit, then back to pasture! His path sounds kind of lackluster at first glance. Before long, with God at his side, he had killed a lion and a bear. Then his righteous anger called him to defeat Goliath and lead the Israelites to defeat the whole Gath family! Eventually, he ran down anyone who dared to defile the Armies of the Living God! If that doesn't get you fired up, nothing will!

When I quit smoking back in 2009, and my team members went out for a smoke break, I used to say quietly to myself, "I'm a nonsmoker, nonsmokers don't smoke." Now we can say, "I am a Believer, Believers don't [fill in with the bad habit you are trying to break]." Then occupy yourself with something productive—or go to bed if you tend to stay up late binge-watching.

The pool or beach are other areas to practice. If you find yourself thinking lustfully, get up and do something active. The ocean is there; go swim in it. Play football with your kids, or play a game with anyone there, make a new friend—and not someone to whom you are physically attracted.

For me, members of the opposite sex were much the source of my previous derailment, but maybe you are purifying yourself from a past same sex attraction. Then obviously you will want to avoid friends that would rekindle that habit.

Not sure about same-sex relationships?

Most people know that decree in the Old Testament, but Paul gives clear guidance on that as well:

> Don't you realize that those who do wrong will not inherit the Kingdom of God? Don't fool yourselves. Those who indulge in sexual sin, or who worship idols, or commit adultery, or are male prostitutes, or practice homosexuality, or are thieves, or greedy people, or drunkards, or are

abusive, or cheat people—none of these will inherit the Kingdom of God. Some of you were once like that. But you were cleansed; you were made holy; you were made right with God by calling on the name of the Lord Jesus Christ and by the Spirit of our God. (1 Cor. 6:9–11)

I realize this is a hotly contested topic these days, but both the Old and New Testaments of God's canonized word, make it clear. I will note that homosexual behavior is no worse than any other sin. Note, Paul includes excessive drinking in the same sentence. Most of what we all struggle with made that list. As a reborn follower of Christ, you are justified from that sin. You must work diligently to sanctify your beliefs and lifestyle to the guidance of scripture. Just like the others, it requires persistent renewal of the mind and perhaps lifelong focus away from that old habit.

> **If someone you know is struggling in an area, be their friend, we are called to make disciples, not enemies**

In this fallen world, everyone has to find Jesus in their own way. If you or someone you know is struggling in this area, be their friend. We are called to make disciples, not enemies. God will give you the words and prayers when the time comes, without you endorsing their lifestyle. Although I'm not an attorney and this is not legal counsel, if you are required to say or do something that goes against the word of God, as of right now, it is perfectly legal to respectfully decline. Here's what Paul says:

> Dear friends, I warn you as "temporary residents and foreigners" to keep away from worldly desires that wage war against your very souls. Be careful to live properly among your unbelieving neighbors. Then even if they accuse you of doing wrong, they will see your honorable behavior, and they will give honor to God when he judges the world. For the Lord's sake, submit to all human authority—whether the king as

> head of state, or the officials he has appointed. For the king has sent them to punish those who do wrong and to honor those who do right. *It is God's will that your honorable lives should silence those ignorant people who make foolish accusations against you. For you are free, yet you are God's slaves, so don't use your freedom as an excuse to do evil. Respect everyone, and love the family of believers. Fear God, and respect the king.* (1 Pet. 2:11–17, emphasis added)

Shadrach, Meshack, and Abednego did a great job of remaining respectful even beyond the moment of being thrown into the fire. Daniel operated with the same respect, as did Esther, Peter, and Paul when confronted by authority figures. Fear God first, then respect the king. Be the light and let God judge them.

Remember, God was the *first* equal opportunity employer. Romans, Greeks, prostitutes, and many others followed Jesus before and after His resurrection. Simon, from Africa, had the distinct honor of carrying His cross! Many assume he was black because of where he was from, but that's not stated specifically, so it's obvious to me that the Holy Spirit didn't think his race was worth noting.

> **Skin color should have no effect on whether you share the Gospel**

Food for thought, skin color should have no effect on your sharing the Gospel.

In Marine Corps Boot Camp, it has been said that we are "all equally worthless" until *earning* the Eagle Globe and Anchor. Jesus' perspective is that we are "all equally priceless" and He gives us a crown to wear. Salvation is a gift. It cannot be earned. He wants us all. As a Jesus following business leader, you need to operate with the understanding that before Christ, everyone was once something else, just like Marines. God's grace was sufficient for you, you need to share it. Live a life that is to be modeled so that others can truly see you are cleansed by the word of the Lord.

Return full circle to being someone whose words and commitments have meaning. The best way to mitigate the tendency for dishonor in our handshakes, agreements, contracts, and covenants is to control our thoughts. Replace them with God's word. Trade up. Instead of radio, listen to a preacher or worship music. Instead of pornography or scrolling Instagram bikini pictures, go for a walk. Instead of waking up and checking email, read a devotional or pray for fifteen minutes.

A deep dive on gates through your body to your soul are beyond the scope of this book, but they are simply the five senses: eyes, ears, nose, mouth, and touch. There is an enemy at those gates, like a roaring lion. Protect those entrances and allow your spirit, which is the Holy Spirit, to have control of your mind, will, and emotions. These are the "senses" or facets of the soul. This ultimately allows the "senses" of the spirit, communion with God, intuition from the Spirit, and your conscience to guide your soul instead of what comes through the physical gates. If you'd like more detail about this topic, please contact me through our website:

JerryHowardInternational.com

Or join our community for free, found at the same location, just click community at the top and join.

Figure 4

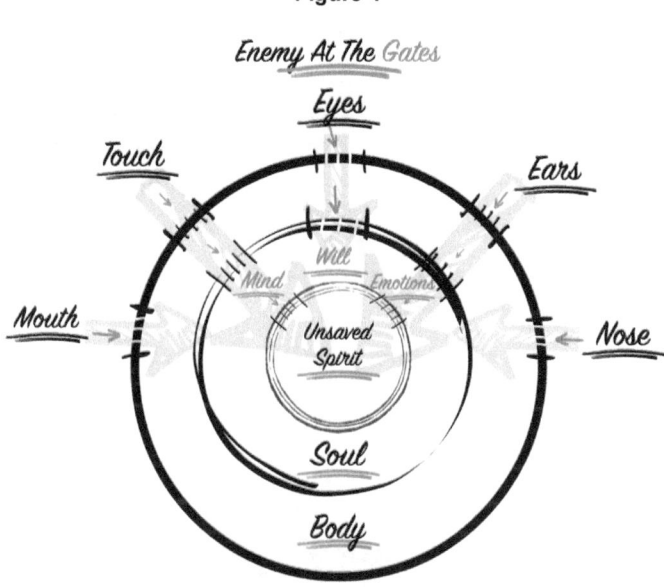

Note. Like an unlocked, empty house, the enemy, Satan has full access to the unsaved spirit.

Figure 4 shows how the enemy is at the gates, twenty-four hours a day, seven days per week. Controlling the gates controls your thoughts. Your external input must be lined up with the spiritual input that is available to you upon submission to Jesus. When all three of these are in alignment, you are operating in the plan and purpose of God. Even when everything around you is crashing down, you are protected. The fruit of this alignment is a peace which transcends all human understanding.

Thankfully, the Spirit of a believer cannot be possessed or controlled by the enemy. According to Romans 8, once you give your life to Jesus, you are justified. Then, sanctification begins. As you shore up the gates to your body, following God's second five rules for life, your soul endures less trauma. As your spiritual senses begin to inform your soul and body, as God intended, that is when the real fun begins!

With body and soul protected, informed by

> **When body, soul and spirit are in alignment with God, and the world is crashing down, you are sealed and protected**

your spiritual senses—intuition, conscience, and communion with God—you become an everlasting spring of Living Water! As Figure 5 reveals, the peace that Jesus commanded you to retain, begins to radiate out to others.

Figure 5

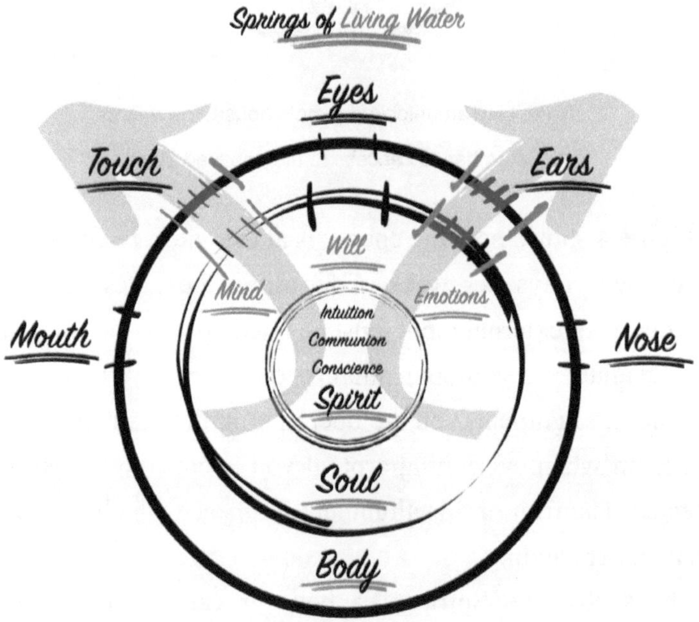

Springs of Living Water

Note. Springs of living water shine a light for all to see.

Supernatural peace is what attracts others to you. Your spirit becomes the ark for those around you. When Noah got in alignment with God's plan by warning others and working on the ark, all the resources, animals, and time needed for completion were supernaturally drawn to him. Alignment is the magnet.

If your actions do not match your words, and especially your covenant with Jesus and your spouse, you will repel others. Remember, you can't have leadership without faith. You can't have people without leadership. You can't have business without people. Faith, leadership, and business are as inseparable as Father, Son, and Holy Spirit. They require the same alignment as your body, mind, and spirit.

Business functions, sales, operations, and finance must be in alignment to achieve the desired outcomes as well. People, now more than ever, want to join something that inspires them to be better than they were yesterday; particularly at work, where they spend so much of their time. They want alignment of their purpose, their dreams, and their work. As a leader in the marketplace, you are behind enemy lines, but are called to be that inspirational light for which people so desperately yearn. Go and make disciples!

If you are not sure of your purpose on this earth, or in Christ Jesus, start with the Big Ten. This book goes beyond just finding your purpose, but doing so is foundational. There are three more of God's ten rules for life for us to cover. The techniques for improving your work life and business operations pivot on God's word. You are the common denominator, thus your use of them to make daily decisions is vital to your walk with the Lord.

The Boardroom or Bible Study

For group discussion and individual journaling:

How does marriage make the world better? Worse?

What do you love most about your spouse/significant other/most trusted family member? How do you show your devotion?

Whether you succeeded or failed, when has honoring your agreements been pivotal to your life?

How do you make friends with people from different cultures? How does that reflect Jesus in you?

When have you felt ashamed or reluctant to share the Gospel, but you knew God was leading? Was it a person or situation? How did you manage it? If not well, how can you do better next time?

When have you felt the world crashing down, yet you were protected? What did you do to manifest that outcome?

CHAPTER 13

THE BIG TEN FOR BUSINESS: LOVE YOUR NEIGHBOR

> "All tyrannies rule through fraud and force, but once the fraud is exposed, they must rely exclusively on force."
> –George Orwell

The United States has done more to spread the Gospel of Jesus Christ in the last 100 years than any other country. Before that, Great Britain wore the mantle. Before that, the Holy Roman Empire. One can clearly track how and why God allowed these countries to prosper. Let's not brush aside the great suffering done along the way, but the Gospel and Jesus' Great Commission is still being transported to all nations, or groups of people.

What if our faith was considered hate speech? Who would fund all of those overseas missions?

Most of the premiere universities were established to teach the Bible in Latin and Greek so that the New Testament could be read in the original languages. Today, many of those same establishments are devoid of God and are well known to be no more than activist indoctrination centers. With the amount of assets under management that each possess, it's no wonder they have gotten off course.

Why teach class when the future of the institution lies in wealth creation?

The product of the organization is not a person who knows how to think and solve problems, the product is a better machine for acquiring more assets. Young, angry, energetic, trained activists without a shred of wisdom spread out far and wide. Throughout the workplace and in the largest institutions, they ensure the current agenda can be funded and distributed at lightning speed around the US and the globe.

Almost immediately following the Hamas and Hezbollah attacks of October 7 and 8, 2023, antisemitic violence spiked in the US. In the year following, it worsened.

> ADL (the Anti-Defamation League) today released the final statistics for antisemitic incidents in 2023, reporting a total of 8,873 incidents of assault, harassment, and vandalism across the country. The total represents a 140 percent increase from 2022—already a record-setting year—and the highest level recorded since ADL started tracking this data in 1979. (ADL, 2024)

Where?

For too long, most of US academia instigates, rather that teach. They are not backing truth and justice. They stand idly by while Jewish students are harassed, threatened, and assaulted. Unfortunately, these challenges are commonplace. The *Wall Street Journal* reported on the incidents at Columbia University:

> One faculty member told an Israeli veteran she had served in an "army of murderers," the report said. Another suggested Israeli military veterans shouldn't be allowed to study on campus. Military service is mandatory for most Israelis. In April, after pro-Palestinian supporters pitched an encampment on the campus, Jewish students reported the antagonism worsened. Protesters shouted, "October seventh is going to be every day for you," in reference to the killing of about 1,200 people by Hamas militants on that day last fall. "People that you sat in class with, you had drinks with, you had lunch and dinner with, the next day they say they hope your entire family dies," one student told the task force. "If I can put it in one word, it is heartbreaking." (Belkin, 2024)

The report noted that three deans were dismissed for antisemitic actions, and that the University President stepped down after less than a year in the position. Almost overnight, Jewish students went from being considered the same as any American minority to being fiercely hated.

Why?

In the last twenty years, these so-called institutions of higher learning around the US have taught students that someone else's success is to their detriment. Critical race theory is the pinnacle of this movement. Students have been taught that it is merely external forces that cause internal turmoil. These institutions have taught young people that if someone has something you want, just take it from them. If your target is bigger, stronger, and has more resources, they are the oppressor, without action or motive. What do the Romans, the Pharisees, and the corrupt institutions of higher learning all have in common?

Theft is okay. To them, stealing in the name of their purpose supersedes the sovereignty of another human being.

God is sovereign. We are made in His image. Therefore, we are sovereign. Freedom is the bedrock of the Founding Fathers' motive to form a new nation, under God. Thus, God's eighth rule for a great life reads:

> You must not steal. (Exod. 20:15)

Stealing begins in the mind. These institutions have one goal: take what is yours. If they can strip your resources, by whatever means, they can enslave you. The actionable phrase to remember is, LOVE YOUR NEIGHBOR.

Sound archaic?

> **LOVE YOUR NEIGHBOR**

Currently in California, robbing a store without taking more than $950 is a misdemeanor, which can carry jail time. Another unmentioned runaway train called *defund the police*, makes prosecution highly unlikely. If left unprosecuted, is it technically wrong?

I own multiple businesses, employ others, and $950 is important to all of us. Some of my team members only make $950 per week! Unequivocally, it is wrong, but a society that does not encourage justice quickly dissolves.

What if a group of minor criminals got slightly organized and robbed the business weekly?

Multiply $950 by each offender times the frequency at which they steal. Multiply that by four or five stores in a small radius. In a year's time, that could be mid-six figures.

The mentality of, might is right, has brought us full circle to the very core of what makes Christians different. During Jesus' time on earth, the Roman Empire was at its strongest. They believed that if you were able to defeat someone in battle, the gods were in your favor—might is right. It didn't stop with the Romans, though. Look at what the disciples asked Jesus about someone he healed:

> As Jesus was walking along, he saw a man who had been blind from birth. "Rabbi," his disciples asked him, "why was this man born blind? Was it because of his own sins or his parents' sins?" "It was not because of his sins or his parents' sins," Jesus answered. "This happened so the power of God could be seen in him. We must quickly carry out the tasks assigned to us by the one who sent us. The night is coming, and then no one can work. But while I am here in the world, I am the light of the world." Then he spit on the ground, made mud with the saliva, and spread the mud over the blind man's eyes. He told him, "Go wash yourself in the pool of Siloam" (Siloam means "sent"). So the man went and washed and came back seeing! (John 9:1–7)

There's quite a bit going on here.

First, as did most Jews at the time, the disciples believed that if someone in your ancestry sinned, then it caused birth defects. It was also believed that if you were wealthy, God considered you righteous, since you carried favor with God and man. Seems logical, but Jesus dispelled that in his explanation of the man's blindness.

Looking back through time, one can correlate the Romans, British, and American prosperity as a function of God's plan to spread the Gospel. All things work according to God's plan.

Is it fair that the blind man was blind? Ask him.

When he was healed, how did he react? Did he blame God for blindness or glorify Him to the community?

Let's read:

> "I don't know whether he is a sinner," the man replied. *"But I know this: I was blind, and now I can see!"* "But what did he do?" they asked. "How did he heal you?" "Look!" the man exclaimed. "I told you once.

Didn't you listen? Why do you want to hear it again? Do you want to become his disciples, too?" Then they cursed him and said, "You are his disciple, but we are disciples of Moses! We know God spoke to Moses, but we don't even know where this man comes from." "Why, that's very strange!" the man replied. "He healed my eyes, and yet you don't know where he comes from? We know that God doesn't listen to sinners, but he is ready to hear those who worship him and do his will. *Ever since the world began, no one has been able to open the eyes of someone born blind. If this man were not from God, he couldn't have done it."* (John 9:25–33, emphasis added)

The blind man glorifies God and doesn't care about the past! Jesus does a few other things worth noting. In the Jewish culture, spit was considered filthy. Dirt was the same. Jesus rubbed nastiness on the guy's face! Not only that, but He did it on the Holy day. The Pharisees had made a mockery of God's guidance for clean and healthy living by their corrupt hearts. Conversely, Jesus made a mockery of them and the hypocrisy for which they stood. They followed the letter of the law, not the spirit of the law.

In the podcast, *Hillsdale Dialogues,* Dr Larry Arnn, President of Hillsdale College, discusses with Hugh Hewitt many important books and topics in history and current events. In one particular episode from December 2023, Dr. Arnn says, "You can believe in goals or rules." He believes in goals. Jesus believed in goals. The goal was for humans to recognize their need for a Savior and reconnect with God through Jesus. By ignoring the spirit of God's sacred law, the Pharisees' idolatry was just as bad as the Romans.

This perspective brings an interesting contrast in the approach of the Pharisees and the Romans. The Pharisees, who claimed to uphold God's sacred laws, had lost sight of the spiritual purpose behind those rules. Their devotion had become a form of idolatry, as as they elevated tradition and rigid observance over the transformative intent of God's commandments. In this way, their idolatry was spiritually hollow, despite being masked by religious zeal.

On the other hand, the Romans were transparent about their objective: the glory and power of Rome. Unlike the Pharisees, they did not pretend to act for spiritual or moral reasons. Their empire's brutal campaigns of murder, pillaging, and oppression were all in service of a singular goal—maintaining Roman supremacy and securing a steady flow of resources, slaves, and tax revenue. For the Romans, it was purely business, plain and simple.

These two groups, though different in their intentions, found common ground in their opposition toward Jesus. His growing influence disrupted their financial networks, heightening their disdain.

Jesus hit them both where it hurt the most. Threatening revenue drove their fear and hate of Him. He no longer allowed the Pharisee's to operate with impunity. He called them out and established His kingdom, not in people's neighborhood, but in their hearts. Peter revealed this impact at the day of Pentecost:

> **Jesus hit them where it hurt the most, threatening their revenue drove their fear and hate of Him**

> "So let everyone in Israel know for certain that God has made this Jesus, whom you crucified, to be both Lord and Messiah!" Peter's words pierced their hearts, and they said to him and to the other apostles, "Brothers, what should we do?" Peter replied, "Each of you must repent of your sins and turn to God, and be baptized in the name of Jesus Christ for the forgiveness of your sins. Then you will receive the gift of the Holy Spirit. This promise is to you, to your children, and to

those far away—all who have been called by the Lord our God." (Acts 2:36–39, emphasis added)

Consistent with Ezekiel's prophecy of:

> And I will give you a new heart, and I will put a new spirit in you. I will take out your stony, stubborn heart and give you a tender, responsive heart. And I will put my Spirit in you so that you will follow my decrees and be careful to obey my regulations. (Ezek. 36:26–27, emphasis added)

At Pentecost, their hearts were pierced and filled with the Holy Spirit.

Where does Jesus elevate God's eighth rule for success? The Jewish leaders had two major systems rolling, one was extorting the Romans with control of the mob. It was wrong to use fear, but it could have been justified if they weren't simultaneously robbing their fellow Jews. The "money changers" as it is written, were declaring sacrificial animals as unclean at the altar. Brought from home or purchased on the way to the temple, the cost was standard. After being declared unclean, the hypocrites' partners would buy the unclean animals at a discount.

Later, and for a massive markup, they would sell the same animals as "preapproved" clean animals to others in the temple. It has been estimated that in today's dollars, the chief priest would have been a billionaire. Here's how Jesus reacted:

> Jesus entered the Temple and began to drive out all the people buying and selling animals for sacrifice. He knocked over the tables of the *money changers* and the chairs of those selling doves. He said to

them, "The Scriptures declare, 'My Temple will be called a house of prayer,' but you have turned it into a *den of thieves!*" (Matt. 21:12–13)

Again, let's answer the question, "What does this have to do with my business or job?"

My executive background was first in healthcare, then construction. Both industries struggle with fraud and theft. Healthcare in America is often pointed at as being broken. That is somewhat true, but its far better than most of the world. The system is still somewhat competitive, which drives innovation and improved patient care. That is the one thing it currently has going for it.

If we completely socialize the whole thing, that is, allow the government complete control of the industry, simple economics predicts disaster.

How?

If competition is eliminated, the incentive for lower costs and improvement vanishes. Value, better care at lower cost, and the incentivization for people to learn the various trades associated with the industry need to remain. It's a hard job, and workers need to be compensated. No competition, no improvement.

As CEO or Administrator, depending on the title used by the controlling organization, I didn't wash the floor, make food, or care for patients. My job was to ensure that five-star clinical outcomes were achieved and revenue and profit goals were reached. I would liaise to the public and facilitate interdepartmental communication.

Simple, right?

Nothing in healthcare is simple. It's all about people, and people are complex. The billing system alone took a huge team. Essentially three massive departments had to work in tandem, just to account for one med pass, meal, or treatment given.

Where is theft occurring?

Theft in healthcare is both overt and subtle. Overt theft is when staff and clinicians steal from facilities. Some level of that exists in every industry. What's unique about healthcare is the subtle theft. Unnecessary treatment is the most glaring. Hospitals and doctors are compensated by care given, nothing wrong there. What happens when they treat someone who doesn't medically need the care?

Since it was one of my runaway trains, let's examine gender reassignment surgery, historically known as a sex change. Although it exists, very few of these surgeries are needed to save someone's life. Many informational sources today will attest to this procedure preventing suicide and a host of other psychosocial issues. However, the most comprehensive longitudinal study examined over 300 patients from 1973 to 2003. Led by Cecilia Dhejne, Department of Clinical Neuroscience, Division of Psychiatry, Karolinska Institutet, Stockholm, Sweden, published in PLOS provides a definitive conclusion:

> Persons with transsexualism, after sex reassignment, have considerably higher risks for mortality, suicidal behaviour, and psychiatric morbidity than the general population. Our findings suggest that sex reassignment, although alleviating gender dysphoria, may not suffice as treatment for transsexualism, and should inspire improved psychiatric and somatic care after sex reassignment for this patient group.

The most significant evidence is that suicide rates for patients increased by nearly twenty times the normal rate for those having undergone this procedure.

What does this have to do with theft?

Stealing one's identity given by God and stealing their possible descendants certainly counts! As was detailed in prior chapters, biologically and psychologically, gender from birth is incorporated in every cell and tissue in the body. It is physically impossible to change them all, lifelong treatment to suppress the birth gender is required to maintain as close to normal life as possible.

What's the incentive to encourage this treatment?

One sex change operation conservatively creates about $40,000 in initial revenue, not including the life-long treatment. Although mortality rates are substantially higher, let's assume you create a new source of revenue for approximately ten years. Between follow-up surgeries, medication, and counseling, long-term revenue can exceed $900,000 per patient. The average number of these surgeries in the US per year is approximately 12,000. Simple math produces $10 billion. That is a significant incentive to encourage treatment and deem it medically necessary. You may recall my personal issue is with this treatment performed on minors.

What if each minor lived twenty years instead of ten?

Medicare and many insurance plans cover these treatments if medical necessity is proven. The participants, that is taxpayers, and those who pay the monthly premiums for insurance foot the bill. Therefore, a significant portion of the population is paying for treatment that has not been proven effective and violates their beliefs. Many doctors and clinicians, in order to protect their livelihood, are required to affirm gender transition for minors.

In general, the most systemic issue with the healthcare system is the fiscal relationship between patient, care provider, and payer. In most cases, the payer is the state or federal government or an insurance company. To achieve maximum allowable charges, providers are incentivized to give treatment, even if it's not needed. In response, the insurance companies simply raise rates. Patients have to pay, or we don't have coverage. In the case of the government raising taxes, we have to pay, or ultimately go to jail.

Theoretically, the cost of care is spread as the healthy people subsidize the care of those less fortunate. This is not horrible, particularly for a first-world country. A healthy population thrives, and we all want the care when *we become* the less fortunate, but the current system promotes treatment rather than preventative maintenance.

Hospitals have become systems, huge conglomerates designed to ensure that every patient stays in their continuum of care, maximizing the margins over a large population. This full continuum of care still has enough players for competition to occur, but it's shrinking. These systems maximize revenue through treatment, not cure.

Doctors are compensated by how many patients they "see" every day. Patients are given the least amount of facetime for which they

> **Compared to private, competing entities, the government is 3 to 10 times less efficient**

can bill. Not the doctor's fault, they have to somehow recoup the hundreds of thousands of dollars they paid for medical school and the multitude of staff required just to correctly bill for services!

Government control is not the answer. For 250 years and prior, large government entities have never proven to be more efficient or effective at overseeing any system. Compared to private, competing entities, the government is predictably three to ten times less efficient. Reducing time to market, regulations on R&D, taxes, and subsidies on care will all bring healthcare costs down. Protecting patients is important. The government should regulate safety, not payment.

What's the cure?

I am certainly not qualified for that hurdle. I can postulate that if the government were to remain in the payment business, they should change how the system rewards the provider. Incentivize a cure, incentivize more value with less cost to the end user, the patient. I'm no billing expert, but logically a cure for less cost is the best outcome for the patient and taxpayer. Patients should be immediately rewarded for better care of their own well-being.

Construction is another theft-heavy industry. The most obvious is the "change order." There are general contractors (GC), who encourage their project managers, through bonuses, to look for ways to make the subcontractors pay for the changes that are made a the project, even if it was the owner or general contractor who initiated it. At the federal level, the US taxpayer foots the bill, not necessarily the subcontractors per se. At the local level, the smallest company, the one with the least amount of wiggle room in his budget, suffers.

How?

Leverage. Larger contractors have the influence to dictate terms. Large manufacturers have the cash and credit to do the same. The subcontractors who want future work will essentially eat it from the general contractor by believing the phrase, "we'll make it up on the next one." That means the GC will hire them for the next job and let that owner pay more, even if unnecessary! Sometimes they do, and sometimes they don't. Either way, the little guy, the *small business*, loses.

Large contractors also like to hold subcontractor payments for as long as they can. If they have a good enough accountant, they can get quite a return on that cash in forty-five, sixty, and ninety days. The problem is, other than the obvious and illegal commingling of funds (I use that term loosely), most vendors or manufacturers require payment in thirty days or less.

At the national level, large firms were notorious for bidding inappropriately on government projects. In the broadest sense, they frequently omitted substantial portions of the scope to achieve more competitive pricing and win the contract. Later, they would look for ways to implement change orders to complete the project correctly. Obviously, this caused massive increases to the American taxpayer. Thinking the government had unlimited resources, as many do, this went unchecked for decades. Thankfully, federal and state governments have implemented increased restrictions in recent years.

Ever wonder why government projects take twice as long and double the budget? Poor ethics and criminal activity. It really is that simple. We all know it, though some of us don't want it to be true. Faith-driven leaders, whether business people or not, should always seek improved efficiency. Until constraints are implemented, there is no incentive to do this. Another word for constraint is budget. Financial educators—all of them—start with this concept.

Is it not logical for federal leaders to do the same? What if at least seventy-five percent of American companies adhered to God's eighth principle for a great life? What if transgressors to this law were held to account?

Billions, trillions of dollars, in wasted revenue would be kept in the pockets of our ever-shrinking working class.

I have big dreams for me, my family, and our posterity. I can understand the desire to grow revenue into the nine and ten figures, but we need to look first to God for the plan. As a believer in Jesus Christ and a follower of His ways, we have the Holy Spirit on the inside of us.

Guess where those big dreams came from?

That's right! God put them there, but as the only One who can see all the dreams at once, He needs to drive the train, otherwise we will be on a collision course that is to end in disaster. Jesus said:

> So don't worry about these things, saying, 'What will we eat? What will we drink? What will we wear?' These things dominate the thoughts of

unbelievers, but your heavenly Father already knows all your needs. Seek the Kingdom of God above all else, and live righteously, and he will give you everything you need. (Matt. 6:31–33)

To fulfill this command, we need to pray to Jesus. As CEO, He gives the guidance. Once we have His plan, we yield to it every day. Simultaneously, we live righteously by following His ten rules for life and business. Eliminating the need and desire to steal from others, we patiently acquire everything we need.

Paul writes to the church in Ephesus a great illustration about what happens in our conversion and why. He says:

If you are a thief, quit stealing. Instead, use your hands for good hard work, and then give generously to others in need. (Eph. 4:28)

God knows your heart and deeds, and those done in secret. Let the public version of yourself match the private you. You can and should live in the overflow. God wants you to have enough to share. That's how we make friends. Friends become followers. Followers become disciples!

And on the day you stand before Him, face to face, you get to hear those wonderful words that all warriors in Christ long to hear from their Commanding Officer. Only he won't say them with a salute, he will pick you up in his arms as the Creator and Master of the universe, holding you high above His head as a proud Father.

Well done, my good and faithful servant. You have been faithful in handling this small amount, so now I will give you many more responsibilities. Let's celebrate together! (Matt. 25:23)

The Boardroom or Bible Study

For group discussion and individual journaling:

Other than confiscating physical property, what are two instances where you may have stolen from your neighbor/coworker? How did you reconcile? If not, will you? How?

When Jesus threatened the revenue supply of His opposition, how did they react? How would you feel if you were in the shoes of the Romans? Pharisees? What would you have done?

How has government inefficiency impacted your life personally? How can you contribute to a solution?

CHAPTER 14

THE BIG TEN FOR BUSINESS: SPEAK ONLY TRUTH

> "The Herdmans were absolutely the worst kids in the history of the world. They lied and stole and smoked cigars (even the girls) and talked dirty and hit little kids and cussed their teachers and took the name of the Lord in vain and set fire to Fred Shoemaker's old broken-down toolhouse."
>
> –Barbara Robinson, *The Best Christmas Pageant Ever*

What if the town simply *affirmed* the Herdmans' behavior? Would they have ultimately burned it all down? Consider recent events in American culture. Consider the burning cities. Consider the runaway trains.

Who has lost the most through our lack of standard? Why are Christian leaders, who know better, allowing it to continue?

Before becoming a Christian, I told many lies. Unfortunately, I was kind of good at it. Following my conversion, I'm sure there were a few, but I continuously strive to behave and have been largely successful. With my kids, two of whom were young when I converted, I didn't lie. If they asked about something I didn't think they were ready to hear, like my very colorful life before Christ—especially drinking, drugs, and jail—I would essentially postpone the conversation. It might go a bit like this.

"Daddy, have you ever done drugs?"

My reply, "Son, Daddy's issues are not your issues, you are a totally different person. So, what's most important is that you do the right thing. Since they are bad, are you going to do drugs?" Of course, they say no. To this day, I have not seen any indication to the contrary.

As they got older, I told them that as they exceeded the age in which my poor decisions were made, I would share with them the stories associated with that time in my life. Two of my children are now in college, and they know some things, but because they are awesome and successful, there may be no reason to "tell all" at any point unless it's relevant to share the wisdom. That has been my determining factor, the sharing of wisdom.

B.C. Jerry, that is, Before Christ, there's no telling. My litmus test was, "can I get away with this?"

Ever since I was little, I realized that I was smart enough to weave my lies together in a simple enough way to maintain the fabrication. Then it became a game. As I grew older, I realized that lying for the sake of doing so was unproductive to my goals; too much to remember.

> **To bear false witness is to use words and actions to project something onto someone's psyche that is not representative of reality**

The filter was, "Do I need this lie to win?" By the time I was thirty, I had spent so much time and energy in a state of falsehood, that I began to develop symptoms of PTSD. This next topic is very near and dear to me, because knowing the truth has consistently brought more freedom as I walk in a growing unity with the Lord's will.

God's ninth rule for a great life was pivotal for me. He says:

> You must not testify falsely against your neighbor. (Exod. 20:16)

This is more than just lying about someone else. To bear false witness in Jerry-speak is, "using words and actions to project something onto someone else's psyche that is not representative of reality."

The actionable approach to this is, SPEAK ONLY TRUTH.

Breaking this down, we need to define "speak" and "truth." As a Christian, you cannot "define your truth," as many of the unsaved insist today. God's word is the only truth. Many today are so insistent on defining their truth that they cannot define a woman. A human female. Done. Science and God agree. Why doesn't the mainstream and academia?

SPEAK ONLY TRUTH

Defining "speak," should be simple. But perhaps it's not as obvious as you think. We know that actions "speak" louder than words. James, Jesus' brother, and later the leader of the church in Jerusalem, says this about action:

> What good is it, dear brothers and sisters, if you say you have faith but don't show it by your actions? Can that kind of faith save anyone? Suppose you see a brother or sister who has no food or clothing, and you say, "Goodbye and have a good day; stay warm and eat well"—but then you don't give that person any food or clothing. What good does that do? So you see, faith by itself isn't enough. Unless it produces good deeds, it is dead and useless. (Jas. 2:14–17)

Here we read that speaking requires more than words.

My definition of speaking might read something like this, "the appropriate use of language validated by corresponding action." In fact, speaking should involve more action than speech. God set this in motion from the very beginning:

> Then God said, "Let there be light," and there was light. And God saw that the light was good. Then he separated the light from the darkness. God called the light "day" and the darkness "night." And evening passed and morning came, marking the first day. (Gen. 1:3–5)

God said a thing and packed His words with faith and power, causing them to manifest a reality. But He didn't stop there. He observed the result of that effort, assessing if it met His perfect standard. He then went to work again. Making it clearer for us, He separated it from the darkness. Then he named it.

God's words, better translated, were, "Light Be!" or "Light Exist!" The corresponding action involved four more steps. He saw it. He assessed its value. He separated it. Finally, He named it. Half of that involved more words, but only as a description for our benefit.

This tells me we need far fewer words to come out of our mouths than we think. No truer words were spoken by someone who speaks and writes for a living! Mostly we need to act. James' example above is a great illustration of too many words and no action. Thus, no impact.

To meet the need of the brother or sister requiring food and clothing, be the one who gives the food or clothing. That's it. Afterward, you will have their full attention. Jesus didn't walk around merely saying, "Follow me." He met people's needs, made a friend, told them how it worked and then asked for their allegiance.

No one will follow you if you don't make a friend. Your job is to lead yourself in a Godly way and let the fruit of that manifest in front of others. Then offer to meet whatever needs of theirs you are able. Jesus' call to Peter was not as simple as most people think, and certainly not an instantaneous conversion! It's a great process for discipleship, detailed later in the book. Speak with action to prove your credibility, then use words to share the Gospel.

Defining truth has been studied for millennia. Philosophically, truth has been marred more than a coin under a moving train! As Christians, we know that God wants us to understand, and therefore, He makes truth simple.

Does anyone completely understand Einstein's theory of relativity?

Probably not, but most of us can remember $E=MC^2$. The reason is, simplicity. As users of this equation, we don't define the terms, Einstein and his predecessors did. Likewise, God's equation for truth is the only one that matters, and the Hebrew language is the best place to start!

A quick disclaimer first: the Monday highlights of a football game have more information than I know about Hebrew. But from what little I do know, the Hebrew language is fascinating! Not only is it phonetic like Spanish and symbolic like Chinese, but it has constructive characteristics. That is, some of its letters are used to create other letters. Let's dive in.

The Hebrew word for truth is *emet*. Emet is formed by combining three letters from the Hebrew alphabet; aleph, mem, and tav, written and read from right to left. There is deep significance to this arrangement. My favorite is the most obvious, that truth encapsulates all. Aleph is the first letter in the Hebrew alphabet, mem is the middle letter, and tav is the last letter. Truth is over all and in all that God has created.

Here's how that looks.

Truth - Emet

Aleph also is the letter that God uses to refer to Himself. Another aspect of aleph is that it is formed with two yods and a vav. These letters represent two hands and a tent peg, hook, or large nail. Thus, God's identifying letter, written at least 1500 years before Jesus went to the cross, was formed by using two hands and a nail. No one foreshadows greatness better than God!

Did that give you chill bumps? If not, read it again.

Mem has many meanings and uses as well, but one is water, specifically the *living water*. Living water represents God's essence permeating all creation. It embodies His divine omnipresence. On the cross, after death, but before His resurrection, Jesus was stabbed. Water released from His heart and lungs.

> One of the soldiers, however, pierced his side with a spear, and immediately blood and water flowed out. (John 19:34)

Water also breaks after pregnancy and before birth. It is what parted for the Hebrews to escape bondage in Egypt, separating slavery and freedom. Water bridged the gap between evil human depravity and Noah's covenant with God. God's essence is bridged by mem, between His name and the final component of truth, or *emet*.

Finally, tav brings the alphabet to a close, representing completion. It seals creation. The seal, or closure, of the work on the cross by Jesus ushered in the New Covenant. He said:

> When Jesus had tasted it [referring to the sour wine], he said, *"It is finished!"* Then he bowed his head and gave up his spirit. (John 19:30, emphasis added)

The Old Covenant was complete with His death on the cross. He fulfilled the sacrifice needed for all of humanity's sin. He reconciled us back to God and at resurrection established the New Covenant. Since Jesus fulfilled one covenant and began the new with His words "It is finished!", we can logically conclude that tav also represents covenant. God's seal, His covenant, and His word are all synonymous.

Using the building blocks of *emet*; aleph, mem and tav, we have both constructed and defined *emet*, or truth. Using God's words, His essence and His action allow Him to define truth as the standard from which all knowledge awakens. His self-identifying words are two hands and a nail, His essence is divine omnipresence, and His action was sealing the covenant.

> **EMET, OR TRUTH: GOD'S DIVINE COVENANT**

What did we build for truth?

God's. Divine. Covenant. The only entity known to man capable of defining truth is God. He embodied this through Jesus and the work of the Holy Spirit. They exist in perfect unity. Jesus specifies to his disciple Thomas here:

> Jesus told him, *"I am the way, the truth, and the life.* No one can come to the Father except through me. If you had really known me, you

would know who my Father is. From now on, you do know him and have seen him!" (John 14:6–7, emphasis added)

God's ninth guideline for a great life is to walk in perfect unity with His word. Stumble we will, but repentance, forgiveness, and restoration will always keep Him close. Fortunately, humility ensures this. No one was more humble than Jesus.

Another use of the letter yod, the hands found in aleph, indicates meekness or humility. Know that meek is not weak. Meek can be illustrated as a trained combat soldier, ready for battle, who chooses to love his enemy instead of destroying them. Again, God defines himself with a double portion of humility. Above all, He expects that from us.

In business, truth should be the standard. Remember, Jesus is CEO. He is the truth. It may be obvious that being true to your word in business is a good idea. As I illustrated in the previous chapter, it so often is not.

How can we *speak only truth* in business?

When your words do not match your actions, you are "bearing false witness." As a Christian leader, you have a higher standard. It takes immense effort to be a person of fortitude in decision-making. With multiple direct reports and hundreds of employees, leaders in the SMB will encounter thousands of competing priorities and obligations. Only God's word will enable us to navigate the chaos safely.

Knowledge of truth, God's Divine Covenant, provides a lens through which decisions are made and actions are assessed. For example, starting your day by listening to God, the people you encounter will either confirm or conflict with His word. Early in my thirties, this simple daily habit brought me a reputation of turning around entire healthcare centers.

How?

Any business leader will have tens or hundreds of people telling their side of an issue. Yet, a decision must be made. God's words about wisdom, his stories about how people mess up, and his goals are the blueprint for success imprinted on our mind. Knowing He's with you when you follow Him provides a supernatural conviction for leading others.

Discernment for truth and fortitude in decision-making are all we need. Changing your mind too frequently due to self-doubt is no different from lying. It creates unrest among your subordinates, and they begin to beat their own drum. Instead of one drum for the operation or company, there are ten, all trying to compete for superiority.

Too much deception will shut down your life operation as well. I believe the weight of lies is like increasing gravity on yourself until you reach a singularity, or a black hole where no light, honor, or truth can emit.

Imagine a smooth bedsheet as you first enter your hotel room. It has no wrinkles. If you were to grab it firmly and twist, it wrinkles to its edges. Navigating to its edges becomes difficult. If you twist further, the sheet begins to knot around your hand, collapsing on itself. Continue, and it can no longer perform as intended.

Lies twist the fabric of reality around you. Your psychological edges become blurry and hard to discern. Our subconscious is great at picking this up. Lies turn you into a ghost of sorts. Becoming unpredictable to your family and team eliminates clarity, even to yourself. Because the fabric of reality around you is so warped, nothing good can emerge, no matter how hard you try. Your

> **Lies twist the fabric of reality, your edges become blurry and morph you into a black hole from which no truth can emerge**

lies morph you into a black hole. Input from others may go in, but nothing they expect comes out.

Before my conversion, this was where my old life ended. I remember leaving the house to buy cigarettes and a police car passed. He didn't pull me over or look in my direction, but I had been in trouble with the law frequently that year. Suddenly my heart rate shot up and I froze. Hands sweating, my fists clenched the steering wheel. I returned home immediately and couldn't leave because of stark terror. I later discovered those were symptoms of post-traumatic stress.

How was I experiencing PTSD? My unit in the Marines was a training command and non-deployable. I never went to combat.

Life in this fallen world is a spiritual war. We are born into combat. Our *Failure Resumé* represents events that produce what I call 'PTSD of life.' The marred coin from the train tracks, my psyche had lived in falsehood for so long that my efforts as a young father of two were also grounded in *pretending*. I was not a good dad. I was so far into the black hole that I didn't realize pure ego was driving my behavior.

Multiple arrests and jail time prompted my sobriety and a hard look at my actions. As a stroke of luck, one of my insurance clients invited me to a series of faith-based business conferences. Each had a Sunday service. It took time, but I finally found my path with the Lord.

After my salvation and later becoming a disciple of Jesus, I reordered my life to faith, family, then finances. Thus, love became my motivation for properly guiding my children through life and later leadership teams in business.

You will have the same impact. Speaking truth into the life of another person will galvanize you in their mind and heart, forever unchangeable. Subsequent interactions solidify that standard, provided you continue to marry appropriate action to your words.

Truth echoes into eternity. Jesus as the way, the truth, and the life accomplished this perfectly according to God's design.

Matt and Alana Grotewald spoke truth about their steadfast faith in God, miraculous family healing experience, and finances as a blessing to bless others on January 24, 2010. I answered their call to accept Jesus as Lord and never looked back. I haven't spoken to either of them since. They live in another state. Yet their words, the words of the Lord, remain.

I stumble today, but humility under Jesus keeps me on track. Those who invited me to that Sunday service continuously spoke the truth about God's love for me. My life still revolves around those truths. Matt's testimony was like a small pebble tossed into a pond. The waves ripple out as far as the pond goes. Were it not for gravity (I know, the pond wouldn't sit, but stay with me), the ripples would continue forever. Truth into someone's life makes a lasting impact.

The Revelation of Jesus gives us license to combine our true testimony, our *Failure Resumé*, especially those events of which we are most ashamed, with His word to overcome any challenge. It reads:

> And they have defeated him *by the blood of the Lamb* and by *their testimony*. And they did not love their lives so much that they were afraid to die. (Rev. 12:11, emphasis added)

Speak only truth. Speak only God's word and your testimony. Then you will walk in victory, for eternity!

The Boardroom or Bible Study

For group discussion and individual journaling:

When have you borne false witness to someone? Did you get away with it? How did you feel?

Would your life look different if you spoke only truth? How?

When have you felt the black hole of your lies closing in on you? How did you escape?

What does God's Divine Covenant mean to you?

CHAPTER 15

THE BIG TEN FOR BUSINESS: APPRECIATE YOUR RESOURCES

> "The time is always right to do what is right."
> —Martin Luther King, Jr.

American Idol. I watched it, same as you. Yet, in our faith, the name should be slightly disturbing.

Itt about sums it up, though, doesn't it?

Groups of people, entire nations, put fame and fortune as the number one pursuit to dominate the airwaves. Living the American dream is life, liberty, and the pursuit of happiness. I agree. I completely agree with the country's Founders and believe that their vision was guided by the Holy Spirit.

Wouldn't it be super cool if we knew what God wanted from us? Just imagine if he sat down with us and gave all the details, beginning to end. He might start with an origin story of some kind, then ...

You get the point, right?

He did. You have purpose. God has a plan. God's ten statements, His ten rules for life, light the path for us.

But Jerry, I can't see around the next turn! What if I go the wrong way?

> He chose me to choose Him—all before the foundation of the world

You won't. You know the beginning, Genesis and Jesus. You know the middle. That's you and God's ten rules for life. You know the end. Go and make disciples until Jesus returns to the earth. Beginning, middle, end.

How do we know He truly wants us?

Good question. I've asked many, many times—even last night! Ugh. Some moments I am just as lost. But there is hope. Jesus is the truth, the life, and the way. He is the only path. He *chose me, to choose Him*—all before the foundation of the world. Jesus makes this abundantly clear in his analogy with Him as the vine. He says it best:

> I no longer call you slaves, because a master doesn't confide in his slaves. Now you are my friends, since I have told you everything the Father told me. *You didn't choose me. I chose you. I appointed you to go and produce lasting fruit*, so that the Father will give you whatever you ask for, using my name. This is my command: Love each other. (John 15:15–17, emphasis added)

He is not unclear.

Most of us think we chose Jesus. Not true. God crafted our lives carefully in our mother's womb, cell by cell, beyond birth, into the world, step by step. Woven into us is a longing for His truth in our hearts. Then one day, we responded to the call … And BOOM! Light

Be! The awakening in our souls was nothing short of explosive. It was celebratory, just as the first words that God spoke into His new universe at 186,000 miles per second so long ago.

Yes, you are that special to Him. You are that important to the cause, and God's mission, the *Missio Dei*, depends on you and me, but it requires focus.

His tenth rule for life, the tenth commandment, underpins the previous four. In fact, one could consider it a capstone for all of them, as it teaches focus. Here are the details:

> You must not covet your neighbor's house. You must not covet your neighbor's wife, male or female servant, ox or donkey, or anything else that belongs to your neighbor. (Exod. 20:17)

If Jesus is CEO and He explicitly tells us to "love each other," then the walking righteous shouldn't be too hard, right?

> **The *Big Ten for Business* control our focus, or attention, in life**

No. For me, the Big Ten make daily decisions infinitely easier. The Big Ten specify where my focus should be at all times. Focus, or attention, is the foundation for the tenth principle for a great life. If we break this one down into parts, we can see the previous four in perfect detail.

"You must not covet your neighbor's house." The only way you are going to obtain my house is to murder me—not kill me, because I would have no reason to fight you (thus creating an opportunity for you to claim self-defense) unless you attacked me in an effort to move me out. That's where I see, "You must not murder," which was number six.

"You must not covet your neighbor's wife." This one is easy. In psychology, we know that we often covet what we see most. Here's the scenario: if you are gazing out the window in Suburbia USA at your neighbor's attractive husband or wife, it won't be long before you slip off into lustful thoughts. Jesus called such thoughts adultery. If a little trouble is brewing in your own marriage, physical adultery is not far from reach.

God then gives some other examples: "male or female servant, ox or donkey, or anything else that belongs to your neighbor." Number eight was, "You must not steal." Coveting your neighbor's property is the first rung in the ladder to stealing it.

Going a step further, once you have done one or all of these things, lying is the only way to avoid immediate prosecution, which leads us to number nine.

From Luke 12:15, we read that Jesus commands us to "Beware! Guard against every kind of greed. Life is not measured by how much you own." And Paul (or perhaps Barnabas) teaches in Hebrews 13:5, "Don't love money, be satisfied with what you have." I'm thinking the same as you.

That's easier said than done, Jerry. How do we mitigate temptation?

God wants our first, middle, and last thoughts to be about Him. Just like *emet*, or truth, He needs to be the first, middle, and last letter of the proverbial alphabet of your life. Paul details this action step in his letter to the Philippians:

> And now, dear brothers and sisters, one final thing. *Fix your thoughts on what is true, and honorable, and right, and pure, and lovely, and admirable. Think about things that are excellent and worthy of praise.* Keep putting into practice all you learned and received from

> me—everything you heard from me and saw me doing. Then the God of peace will be with you. (Phil. 4:8–9, emphasis added)

Jesus is the only *way* to stop worrying about everyone else. By closing our eyes to pray we are "fixing our thoughts." When those urges erupt in our soul, we pray. Eyes closed, we cannot covet. I realize Paul intended the word "fix" to mean "set," but it's likely no coincidence that this also "fixes" a problem. Jesus gave a great example of how he walked by faith:

> So Jesus explained, "I tell you the truth, the Son can do nothing by himself. *He does only what he sees the Father doing.* Whatever the Father does, the Son also does. For the Father loves the Son and *shows him* everything he is doing. In fact, the Father will show him how to do even greater works than healing this man. Then you will truly be astonished. (John 5:19–20, emphasis added)

Jesus' heart was part of the triune God—the Father, Son, and Holy Spirit. If the Father asked Him to go to the cross, then perfect unity demanded perfect compliance.

Just as an officer gives an order to a soldier, the soldier's actions represent the thoughts and intention of the issuing officer. Therefore, the soldier does only what he *sees* his commander order.

Another perspective is through prayer. Jesus spent a great deal of time alone in prayer with the Father. In my prayer time, God gives me insights and ideas. In prayer, Jesus was probably shown glimpses of what must be done.

Glimpses into the future are what all of us do when we need to think about our next steps. For me, I often read His word a bit and stare toward the sky and treetops outside my office window. I'm gazing with my eyes open, but my mind is showing me other images.

Other times, I'll read God's word and think of an idea for applying it in my life or the life of others. *The Big Ten for Business* idea came from one such time in fasting and prayer. I believe this is both supernatural and normal acts of envisioning a reality that has not yet manifested.

Referencing the first commandment again, Jesus is CEO, we are to look only to Him for the next play. Reading His word and prayer are paramount to staying on His path for our lives. We should replace our desires for earthly things with those that are spiritual.

Paul's first letter to the church at Corinth specifies, "So you should earnestly desire the most helpful gifts." Be careful here as we do not want to falsely claim the manifestation of spiritual gifts, but it is consistent with what we learned earlier about "seek[ing] first the kingdom ..." (1 Cor. 12:31, Matt. 6:33).

What about my mind, will and emotions?

Likewise, in prayer, I'm calmed from anxiety, by thinking only of the Father. It is especially effective if you "put [God] in remembrance; [He says], let us argue together; set forth your case, that you may be proved right" (Isa. 43:26, ESV).

God wants you to pray His word, so you can be right, and righteous, at the same time!

How loving is that?

Think about your challenge, or goals, find God's promise relating to that issue, then use His word to make your case. With His word, you win!

Try it, pray for God's next steps in the *Missio Dei*, and simultaneously covet that new Harley you want. It's impossible. And childish. I know, I still do it too. Leaders, the Harley will manifest as the mission is fulfilled. That is called living in the overflow. More on that after we arrest this constant covetousness in our lives. Later in the book, we will explore what God's favorite KPIs are and learn a plan to reach His goals.

Covetousness is rampant in my life, and for many, particularly here in America. Hence names like, *American Idol*. Even writing this book, I had to screen it through my covetousness filter.

Am I writing to obtain fame? Be an expert? Or am I using writing, an activity I find enjoyable, to teach God's word?

I enjoy writing, but publishing a book is incredibly laborious, so I assumed it was the last choice.

Here's my logic. I started writing over ten years ago when I was a stay-at-home dad. Writing about that experience was just an off the wall comment my wife suggested. The idea seemed fun, so I did. Off I went! Over the years, I've gotten graduate level writing training and won a few contests. I've been published four times in small publications, done some editing, and have been a contributing author in many instances. I'm certain God used these experiences to pull me further into the craft.

Writing today has become a passion and a therapeutic antidote to feelings of burnout, loneliness, and uselessness. Writing entered my life at the recommendation of someone, another Christian, whose opinion I trust. It wasn't a marketing tool. I had never written anything consistently except papers for school, so I'm sure this gift fully manifested at my salvation.

What about the content?

The filter is, I have always been a business person. Today, I'm one who has loved God's word since the day I made Jesus Lord. I've always been a student

> **He is always with you, but if you want God's blessing on an activity or pursuit, it needs to be part of His plan and calling on your life**

of leadership, as far back as high school. The intersection of faith, leadership, and business lands right on me—no ego, just a unique *Failure Resumé*, God's word and the talent He gave me!

God is always with you, but if you want His blessing on an activity or pursuit, it needs to be part of the call to which you are appointed. That is called His *anointing*, and favor follows it. You can't just look at another speaker or author and say, "God, please make me like them."

Beware! That is closer to using His name in vain than cursing with it! You are unique and wonderful. Your purpose is specific to you and will not be seen anywhere else on earth. It's only through the lens of Jesus that you can clearly see what He called you.

I believe it is much harder for business leaders to avoid covetousness. In business, you will be surrounded by competitors and industry standards, P&L goals, departmental outcomes, recruitment and retention, morale—this list of metrics is infinite! We are behind enemy lines every day trying to answer God's call and decide which bill to pay or which boss to please. We walk down the hall, drive out of the office park or industrial square and are hammered with grass-is-greener circumstances.

How do we fight this tendency?

> **APPRECIATE YOUR RESOURCES**

In business, I say God's tenth guideline for a great life is, APPRECIATE YOUR RESOURCES. I struggle with this. I got my MBA with a specialization in marketing, so I understand the value of market analysis. The analysis can give you insight into consumer demand, blue and red markets, and what direction to pursue.

Ask yourself why you are walking a certain path. Coveting the ten-figure business owner's lifestyle when yours is six will not bring you closer to fulfillment. You have no idea his or her struggles. They may be so deep in darkness, you wouldn't trade it for Elon Musk's budget. Or worse, you acquire the nine figures, but without wisdom, use it for evil. Ask the tech billionaires and their executives if they regret what social media has done to our children. None of them had children when they designed the algorithms.

Covetousness can lead you away from the purpose of your proximity too. Reading an article or watching a TV show is one way to covet the rich.

What if you do know them personally?

Most people clamor for time to know a wealthy person's secret formula or get a slice of their pie. You might be the special agent God needs to get in there and ask, "How's your soul?" What if you came in asking, "Can I pray for you?" How about, "What keeps you up at night?" Immediately, you stand out as someone different. Here's your reply, "What do you know about Jesus?" God's blessing will flow in ways you cannot imagine!

God is CEO. You know His mission, go and make disciples. His vision is that all would be baptized in the Holy Spirit. His values are the Big Ten. You are ready.

To protect your five body gates, the five physical senses, let's review the latter five policies in God's value statements, and we can wrap up *The Big Ten for Business*. Listed in Figure 6, they are: Respect Human Life, physically and in your mind, Cherish Your Spouse, similarly in business you need to Honor Agreements, Love Your Neighbor, Speak Only Truth, and Appreciate Your Resources.

Figure 6

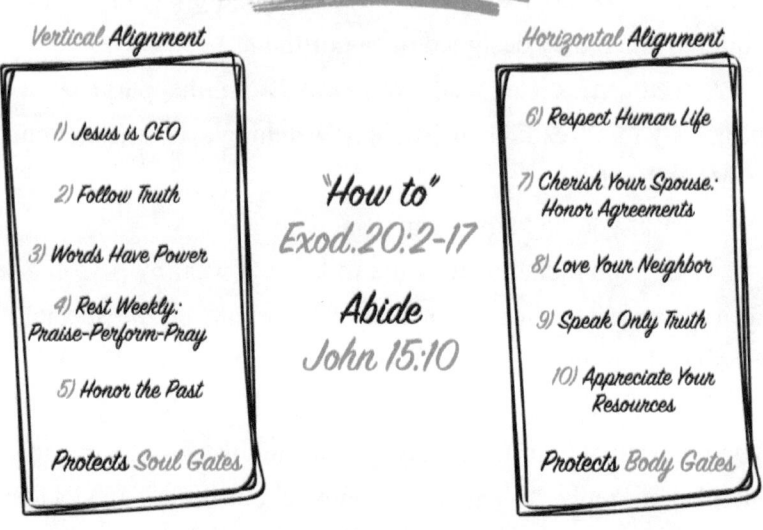

Note. God's ten value statements protect your body and soul.

Now it's time to transform your resources and all of your assets into an engine for discipleship. Carefully watching what the Father does and carrying that out is what being led by the Holy Spirit is all about. Jesus healed the sick, cast out demons, and raised the dead. You can too!

Overcoming obstacles through relying on God, living out His value statements every day, will take you from pain to promotion. With the right approach, you can lead others to a closer relationship with the Lord, while in the midst of challenge. Our next few chapters provide simple metrics that you can use to run any business God's way!

The Boardroom or Bible Study

For group discussion and individual journaling:

Does your life look different than what you think God wants for you? How? What do you need from Him?

What is your current pursuit in life? Are you diligently pursuing it? If so, what is the fruit? If not, what can you change immediately?

What impact would it create in your life if you gave the Big Ten for Business 100 percent focus?

Which of the Big Ten is the most challenging for you? Why?

What resources has God blessed you with? What do you use them for?

PART IV

HOW TO, FOR YOUR TEAM: LEAD OTHERS TO VICTORY

So let's not get tired of doing what is good. At just the right time we will reap a harvest of blessing if we don't give up.

-Galatians 6:9

CHAPTER 16

GOD'S FAVORITE KPIs: THE QUANTITATIVE

> "Data is like garbage. You'd better know what you are going to do with it before you collect it."
> –Mark Twain

For a business that to be world-class, certain pragmatic conditions have to be met. In our faith, God's KPIs are eternally and equally important. God's favorite three KPIs start with how many people have you introduced to Jesus? How many have you begun to apprentice, or taken on as a disciple? And how many lives have been changed because of the relationship you all have with Jesus? Simply put, Jesus wants lots of family members, lots of students, and lots of raving fans.

God's world-class business KPIs, which will make you an industry leader and most effective for building His kingdom, are not based on company size. Remember, world-class businesses can have five employees or 5,000. World-class business is not found only in those listed on NASDAQ or the S&P.

If everyone involved is getting what they need and want, within reason, then the company is world-class. Here's the litmus test.

> **Jesus wants lots of family members, lots of students and lots of raving fans; those are His favorite KPIs**

Are the owner and other leaders available to truly lead others? Are the customers getting what was promised for their money? Are the employees and stakeholders getting what was promised to them for their time and trust?

To achieve world-class, the CEO should be managing seven KPIs, only some of which are financial. We will take a close look at each later, but they are:

1) Percent revenue growth proportionate to profit

2) Percent diversification of revenue

3) Recurring revenue percentage

4) Customer satisfaction

5) Employee engagement

6) Giving percentage of EBITDA

7) Personal wellness

Why aren't God's KPI's *more* important?

While you work on His KPIs, you must properly steward the people and resources that He's already given you. Get your heart and head right. We've covered what you need for that: Follow The *Big Ten for Business* to ensure you and your people are becoming their best. God cares about all your needs, spiritually, mentally, and physically. Jesus says:

> So do not worry, saying, 'What shall we eat?' or 'What shall we drink?' or 'What shall we wear?' For the pagans run after all these things, and *your heavenly Father knows that you need them*. But seek first his kingdom and his righteousness, and all these things will be given to you as well. (Matt. 6:31–33, NIV, emphasis added)

He reminds us that we are not to fret about tomorrow and how we will manage. We also read that our "heavenly Father knows that [we] need these things."

God, from the lips of Jesus, is agreeing that these needs are important, so important that He makes them a priority. Thus, using God's blueprint to create a system that meets those needs is equally important to creating your system for making disciples. To repeat an old Greek proverb for building a great society, paraphrasing, we must plant a tree whose shade we will never enjoy. Solomon adds:

> A good person *leaves an inheritance for their children's children*, but a sinner's wealth is stored up for the righteous. (Prov. 13:22, NIV, emphasis added)

Your business system is the legacy for the next operator of your department, for the buyer of your company, or for generational wealth if you secure it as an asset.

Systems create three things. First, a system drives consistency. A system for your department establishes clear expectations everyone can work under. They know what winning is and how to get there. A system for income in your business, with your profit goals appropriately built in, will bring consistency in your family budget.

Second, a system capitalizes on your intelligence, not your hours. Whether you are the owner, CEO, or site supervisor, if every action requires your input and decision-making authority, you become a bottleneck. A bottleneck in decision-making strangles creativity, burns up resources, and disempowers teams. No bottlenecks!

People are not cheap. Don't waste them! My graduate school business professor used to tell us that our biggest expenses will be rent and employees, and to avoid them both if we could. Since you do have team members, and I believe they are a worthy investment, don't stifle the talent you worked so hard to recruit!

If you are the bottleneck, your problem is one of three things—or all of them. Perhaps you want to be the center of attention. Maybe your self-worth depends on everyone running to you. Equally possible, you do not trust your people to make decisions. If this fits, you are barely managing the company, much less leading it.

Leaders succeed. Be that. If you don't know what that looks like, then follow the previous chapters of this book and you'll get it right. If you have the budget for it, hire me and/or one of my team members to teach you.

Take a hard look at why you don't have systems. Why do all the decisions come from you? You can name thousands of external influences, but they are not the root cause. The problem is internal. When you let go and let God, He celebrates and gets to work! You get to rest. Ultimately, everyone wants peace of mind. It's all in God's blueprint. Jesus guarantees it:

> I am leaving you with a gift—peace of mind and heart. And the peace I give is a gift the world cannot give. So don't be troubled or afraid. (John 14:27)

Our hope rests in the promise of eternal life with Jesus. Before that happens, we get to participate in the installation of that hope in others. Through every occurrence of obedience to that endeavor, our own faith builds, increasing the level of peace with which we walk. Even a mustard seed of faith can move a mountain. Imagine what you can do in an entire organization overflowing with it!

In business, systems plus consistency equals profit. In eight to twelve quarters (2–3 years) a company, regardless of size, can improve dramatically, and bring peace to everyone involved. One of the most frequent topics in the Bible is that of money. He wants us to be well-intentioned and well-resourced. Relinquish the idea of *your* money, adopt a mindset of stewarding *His* resources.

There was gold in the garden of Eden. Abram was well stocked when he left home, and he stayed profitable throughout his journey. Genesis reveals:

> **Relinquish the idea of your money, adopt a mindset of stewarding His resources**

> So Abram departed as the LORD had instructed, and Lot went with him. Abram was seventy-five years old when he left Haran. He took his wife, Sarai, his nephew Lot, and all his wealth—his livestock and all the people he had taken into his household at Haran—and headed for the land of Canaan. (Gen. 12:4–5)

Later, after getting Sarai back from Pharaoh, God ensured his wealth grew:

> So Abram left Egypt and traveled north into the Negev, along with his wife and Lot and all that they owned. (Abram was very rich in livestock, silver, and gold.) (Gen. 13:1–2)

Profit isn't everything; God is everything. Jesus warned about storing up treasures on earth:

> Then he told them a story: "A rich man had a fertile farm that produced fine crops. He said to himself, 'What should I do? I don't have room for all my crops.' Then he said, 'I know! I'll tear down my barns and build bigger ones. Then I'll have room enough to store all my wheat and other goods. And I'll sit back and say to myself, "My friend, you have enough stored away for years to come. Now take it easy! Eat, drink, and be merry!" But God said to him, 'You fool! You will die this very night. Then who will get everything you worked for?' Yes, a person is a fool to store up earthly wealth but not have a rich relationship with God." (Luke 12:16–21)

Put God first, praise Him for what you have, then focus on being prudent with your resources, as God directs. This is Godly. God's system brings peace with Him and man. Peace of mind frees you to help others. Helping others is how you abide in the Lord.

If you are a business leader, the importance of systems should be no surprise. Even the apostles needed systems when growth was hindering delivery of the Gospel message. Luke writes:

> But as the believers rapidly multiplied, there were rumblings of discontent. The Greek-speaking believers complained about the Hebrew-speaking believers, saying that their widows were being discriminated against in the daily distribution of food. So the Twelve called a meeting of all the believers. They said, "We apostles should spend our time teaching the word of God, not running a food program. And so, brothers, select seven men who are well respected and are full of the Spirit and wisdom. We will give them this responsibility. Then we apostles can spend our time in prayer and teaching the word." (Acts 6:1–4)

Everyone liked this idea, and they chose the following to manage the system:

> Stephen (a man full of faith and the Holy Spirit), Philip, Procorus, Nicanor, Timon, Parmenas, and Nicolas of Antioch (an earlier convert to the Jewish faith). These seven were presented to the apostles, who prayed for them as they laid their hands on them. So God's message continued to spread. The number of believers greatly increased in Jerusalem, and many of the Jewish priests were converted, too. (Acts 6:5–7)

This passage illustrates the importance of establishing your team's personality strengths. I like the motivational gifts from Roman's 12 for job alignment, but there are a myriad of psychometrics and personality assessments that are effective.

Please note, when discussing profitable systems, I use profit here loosely. If you are working in a nonprofit, what is your desired outcome?

It could be an increase in donations or maybe more constituents served. If you are leading a small team or department, "profit" to you may be a certain amount of widgets produced or lowering the amount of infections in your healthcare wing. Decide now what winning is, and push authority for decision-making down to the lowest level.

> **CEOs, owners, get your dollars and cents squared away, delegate everything except what only you can do, and get to work for God**

CEOs, owners, get your dollars and cents squared away, delegate everything except what only you can do. Get to work for God—not in the church—right there in your business! Working for God in business is also exemplified by Jesus. To systematize discipleship, structure your time the way He did. Identify your top three apprentices.

Who are your Peter, James, and John?

Keep an eye out for another nine with potential. Make time to apprentice them. Contract trainers like my team to teach seventy more on decision-making. Keep the multitudes fed and excited about what they are doing with great pay and community involvement.

Jesus mentored his top twelve guys. The others followed, but those twelve were His disciples. Systems for this are important. If you lead 1,000 people to the Lord, but have no process for discipleship both at work and partnered with your local church, you may end up fruitless. Chances are, they become like the seed on stony ground or amongst the thorns. To illustrate, Jesus' parable reads:

> Listen! A farmer went out to plant some seeds. As he scattered them across his field, some seeds fell on a footpath, and the birds came and ate them. Other seeds fell on *shallow soil with underlying rock*. The seeds sprouted quickly because the soil was shallow. But the *plants soon wilted* under the hot sun, and since they didn't have deep roots, they died. Other seeds *fell among thorns that grew up and choked* out the tender plants. Still other seeds fell on fertile soil, and they produced a crop that was thirty, sixty, and even a hundred times as much as had been planted! (Matt. 13:3–8)

Confusing to most, Jesus explained to His disciples what he meant:

> The seed on the *rocky soil* represents those who hear the message and immediately receive it with joy. But since *they don't have deep roots, they don't last long*. They fall away as soon as they have problems or are persecuted for believing God's word. The *seed that fell among*

> the thorns represents those who hear God's word, but all too quickly the *message is crowded out by the worries of this life and the lure of wealth*, so no fruit is produced. (Matt. 13:20–22, emphasis added)

A system for discipleship is paramount to your company and the Kingdom.

I noted previously that after I gave my life to the Lord on January 24, 2010, I never saw the business owner who did the altar call and his family in person again. I followed them online for a while, but the people who invited me to the service are the ones who discipled me. Then I plugged into a local church, got baptized, and began attending training classes. I've been learning ever since!

Hope Point Church in Chesterfield, VA, is my home church and has over 100 connect groups, many of which are deep doctrinal classes taught by the founding pastors, the lead pastors, and the elders. Many are online and open to all, come check us out!

To keep our hearts and teams fertile, we must foster an atmosphere of apprenticeship. Everyone, especially the younger generations, desperately wants to be the best version of themselves. In the marketplace, leaders have them forty to fifty hours per week. Let's make it count!

With that said, the marketplace is full of miracles. When Jesus healed the sick, cast out demons, and raised the dead, he was typically in the marketplace.

How might that look in your workplace?

Getting your leadership team healthy will immediately bring healing to anyone

> **Getting your teams in alignment brings immediate healing; when people work the way they were created, work becomes play**

involved. When people get to work the way they were created, *work becomes play*.

Not to overlook the work of the Holy Spirit, but hat's how we can heal the sick, will you?

When everyone knows how much they complement someone else's weaknesses, toxicity, backstabbing, unhealthy, competitive behavior vanishes.

Does that sound like casting out demons?

When people actually appreciate the other members of their family and teams, relationships are restored.

Would you say those relationships are raised from the dead?

The spirit between two people taps into what Napoleon Hill called Infinite Intelligence. The third entity produced by the love and activity between God the Father and His Son, Jesus, is the Holy Spirit. When two people are working toward the same goal, in the way they do best, they have the same impact. Jesus said:

> Again, truly I tell you that if two of you [Believers] on earth agree about anything they ask for, it will be done for them by my Father in heaven. For where two or three gather in my name, there am I with them. (Matt. 18:19–20, NIV)

That same Spirit raised Jesus from the dead! God's number one goal for Jesus was to restore the broken relationship with us. That is all He wants. When you restore relationships using God's blueprint, you are walking in perfect unity with Him.

To truly operate your team, department, or business as its COO, it requires being *proactive*. If all you do is put out fires all day, you are *reactive*. It may take anywhere from 12–36 months, but with intentionality, you can chip away at your reactionary habits bit by bit. Start by managing God's seven KPIs. Three years is not very long for profit and peace.

Profit Growth Exceeds Revenue Growth

First, are your financials. If you have outside funding, great. I say work toward ultimately becoming your own bank. Your surplus of revenue from the systems you create produces profit. Every month, you should be comparing *revenue growth percentage to profit growth percentage.* If your revenue growth rate exceeds your profit growth rate, you are growing too fast, and you will run out of cash.

I like to keep profit growing at a slightly faster rate than revenue. This tells me that I am either getting more for less or producing the same with less effort, or expense.

This may seem obvious, but how many CEOs, particularly in the SMB, actually manage this?

You'd be surprised how few. Chasing revenue at the expense of profit was my first issue as a new business owner. It took a few years of robbing Peter to pay Paul (pun completely intended) for me to realize that I was killing both the company's future and myself. Through acquisition and marketing strategies, we did grow to six-fold our initial revenue, but our margins were barely in the black—and sometimes red! I think part of me was pursuing revenue just so that I could say I did. Ugh. What's worse, I was well into my Christian walk, still driven by godless ego!

> **If revenue growth exceeds profit growth, you will run out of cash**

Growth for growth's sake is not Godly. After the fall, over thousands of years, God typically worked through one man until Joseph. Abraham was his guy, then Isaac, then Jacob. Jacob's sons, including Joseph, headed up the twelve tribes of Israel. Revealing His glory, God grew the nation quickly, in spite of great oppression in Egypt. His system's foundation, righteousness through faith, was in place first through Abraham and his whole house.

I personally believe that the Hebrews became enslaved because they stopped telling themselves and the Egyptians how they got there, why they were saved from famine, and what God did through Joseph to make Egypt the most powerful country the earth had yet to see.

When in the wilderness, we repeatedly see the Hebrews' desire to return to slavery, even after the ten plagues and the Red Sea crossing. I'm certain that's why God chose to raise Moses in the finest Egyptian palace, so he could become a learned man and finally write God's word down. Creation, the fall, the flood, Abraham and his posterity needed to be enshrined in a *Book of Instruction*. Moses, under the Spirit of the Lord, ensured they could refer back to the Law when they got off track. Good thing too!

Like all of us, the Hebrews consistently needed to return to God's word with humility to get out of trouble. God warned them in Deuteronomy, they have a choice, every day. Pursue your goals, like more revenue for revenue's sake, and face destruction. Or choose God's path. He writes:

> Today I have given you the choice between life and death, between blessings and curses. Now I call on heaven and earth to witness the choice you make. Oh, that you would choose life, so that you and your descendants might live! You can make this choice by loving the LORD your God, obeying him, and committing yourself firmly to him. This is the key to your life. (Deut. 30:19–20)

Bottom line: profit gives you options. Profit over time makes you a better instrument in the marketplace for the Lord's work. Do not let anyone tell you profit is bad. Ever.

You wouldn't believe how many owners and CEOs take on what I call bad revenue. Bad revenue is a contract that requires too many one-offs in your systems or one with margins below your goal. I promise, you won't make it up on the next one. Bad revenue is that which pushes you over your diversification limit as well. That is our next world-class metric.

Diversification of Revenue

Diversification of revenue is ensuring that none of your revenue is sourced from a single contract, license, or vendor agreement. In *Built to Sell*, John Warrillow teaches that ideally, not one customer will exceed fifteen percent of your total revenue. In B2C, this is usually not too hard, but B2B can get tricky. God believed this as well. All of His top people, particularly those in the Old Testament, had multiple sources of revenue from their craft.

This is not to say you should have 15 different LLCs as you may have read or heard. Focusing on one thing until you can automate the revenue from it will produce the most fruit. Jacob was a shepherd, so he had multiple revenue streams from

> **All of God's top people, particularly in the Old Testament, had multiple sources of income**

that endeavor. Farmers have multiple crops. Elon Musk had Paypal, Gates had Microsoft. You get the point. Get one thing done really great, then do other things if you feel called. Diluting your time, energy and resources will only lead to mediocrity in many things. It can potentially cause you to scorn the very thing in which God needed you to excel. Listen to His voice and you will win.

In all the Bible, Jacob is the best example of the true human and God's mercy. Jacob was a liar and swindler and suffered for it.

God still blessed him with intelligence and revenue from diversified sources:

> Whenever the stronger females were ready to mate, Jacob would place the peeled branches in the watering troughs in front of them. Then they would mate in front of the branches. But he didn't do this with the weaker ones, so the weaker lambs belonged to Laban, and the stronger ones were Jacob's. As a result, Jacob became very wealthy, with large flocks of sheep and goats, female and male servants, and many camels and donkeys. (Gen. 30:41–43)

The best way to manage diversification of revenue is knowing that landing the whale isn't always best for your company.

I'm not saying that you cannot sign that dream contract, just be prepared to find another one equally large, with a goal of having no less than seven active at one time. Before the Covid shutdowns, fifty percent of the revenue in one of our companies was from two contracts. Initially, to us who were naïve, this made the company worth purchasing.

Despite having verbal agreements on several, equally large, future projects, Covid's severe economic uncertainty resulted in multiple cancellations or postponements. Thus, fifty percent of our projected revenue for the following 18 months, and beyond, evaporated. Our profit was not ideal as we had just purchased the company. Even if we had thirty percent margins, no one could have predicted the pandemic. As I noted previously, we shut the company down, but I'll never forget to diversify my revenue again, regardless of the industry.

God diversifies. It appeared that God bet on Adam and lost, but in His perfect wisdom, He grew His family to millions to ensure that His bloodline was secure. Through generations, from Seth to Noah to Abraham to David to Jesus, our future was secure. He made sure both Mary and Joseph could trace lineage to David. Jesus' perfect arrival was a diversified approach to blessing billions of people.

Recurring Revenue

God's next KPI is *recurring revenue*. Jesus gave twelve men His *way of living* and His Spirit for empowerment. They distributed this way of living to thousands of others who have created billions of Christ-bearers, or Christians. God's system is not only recurring, but it multiplies!

Does your system recur automatically? Does it multiply?

Every year, I attempt to create more ways for recurring revenue. This is a huge weakness for our first company, which is in construction. If we are not selling, we do not collect. In the residential space, it's one and done, and we work diligently to get referrals and five-star reviews. In the commercial sector, we have about thirty clients who purchase repeatedly from us, so we are well diversified, and they are happy. Although heavily dependent upon commercial activity, I can safely say our recurring revenue percentage is over forty percent.

In our consulting company, we are 85–90 percent recurring, which is what attracted me to the business model. In addition, it aligns with my leading, Romans 12 motivational gifts: teaching, encouraging, and administration (leading). My recommendation is to have as much recurring revenue as possible. You can offer subscriptions, service plans, or SaaS.

Another approach, similar to my contracting company, is to gain raving fans that are repeat customers. Maybe you can make revenue multiply independent of you personally, like selling video training courses or writing a book. Remember, God wrote one too!

> ### The Boardroom or Bible Study
>
> *For group discussion and individual journaling:*
>
> *Which one of God's favorite KPIs—more family members, more disciples, and more raving fans—is your favorite? How would your family, team, department, or company change if all three were your favorite?*
>
> *What would it look like if you were just a steward of God's resources? How would you treat your family, time, and money differently?*
>
> *Whether CEO or team lead, how can you delegate your way to being more available for God? Who are you sure will step up? Who will benefit most?*
>
> *Where have you worked that seemed more like fun with a family vs. toiling away for a paycheck? What was the most differentiating characteristic?*
>
> *In a nonprofit organization or individual team or department, what would it look like to "run out of cash?" How would you solve that problem?*
>
> *As a leader, but perhaps not business owner, how can "multiple sources of revenue" be relevant to you? What is the one area where you know God needs your gifts?*

CHAPTER 17

GOD'S FAVORITE KPIs: THE QUALITATIVE

> "Things don't matter equally. Success is found in doing what matters most."
> –Gary Keller

Leadership is a science. There are thousands of step-by-step plans with any number of boxes to check for leading with success. World-class business is a science. Some estimate there are hundreds of KPIs that ensure a successful organization. The soft skills (qualitative) in leadership and business are extremely important to productivity and profit (quantitative). Both are an art. Most importantly, they matter to God. Shifting away from hard financial data is important if you are sincerely attempting to lead well.

Customer Satisfaction

God's next KPI for world-class business is *customer satisfaction*. Measurements for this have become highly effective in the digital age. In B2C, five-star reviews are popular and easy to find. In the B2B, Net Promoter Score is effective but varies widely based on industry. It is less known and there is a general variance on what is considered good for this benchmark. The rule of thumb is simple, score anything above zero. Still valuable, customer acquisition costs can be predicted with this information and a dropping star rating can predict repeat customer loss.

How does God measure customer satisfaction?

Some might say through pain and suffering, others might say from praise, but we are commanded to remain joyful and praise Him through the suffering. This is a fallen world. Jesus said there would be tribulation, but fear not, for He has overcome it. We are commanded *not* to fear.

God measures customer satisfaction through faith. If you are scratching your head right now, hang in there. From the author of Hebrews, we are told:

> Faith shows the reality of what we hope for; it is the evidence of things we cannot see. Through their faith, the people in days of old earned a good reputation. By faith we understand that the entire universe was formed at God's command, that what we now see did not come from anything that can be seen. (Heb. 11:1–3)

Andy Stanley defines faith as "Believing God is who He says He is and that He will do what He says He will do." More from Paul:

> And it is impossible to please God without faith. Anyone who wants to come to him must believe that God exists and that he rewards those who sincerely seek him. (Heb. 11:6)

Skipping a few verses, He wraps up the Faith Hall of Fame with:

> All *these people earned a good reputation because of their faith*, yet none of them received all that God had promised. For God had something better in mind for us, so that they would not reach perfection without us. (Heb. 11:39–40, emphasis added)

In the letter to the Hebrews, we read that faith *pleases God*. If pleasing God is the goal, then He is the customer. His satisfaction is our goal.

> **If pleasing God is our goal, then He is the customer, your faith is His satisfaction rating**

Too many humans think God is supposed to please us. Jesus is CEO, God is the Creator, and we are *His* workmanship. We please Him. Your belief through all circumstances reveals one thing, despite how fallen this world is, you still believe. That is how you are evaluated.

God measures satisfaction through faith, but so do your customers, employees, clients, stakeholders, and partners. Five-star ratings reveal that your customers have faith you will treat their friends and others the same as you did them. The free market operates on faith. We vote in whom or what company we have the most faith every day with our bank account.

We believe that if someone does wrong, the civil tort system will hold them to account and provide recompense. That system is entirely dependent on faith. The purpose of this book is to excite, alarm, and educate marketplace Believers on how important our activities and daily decisions are to remaining free. Faith is the substance hoped for.

I hope for raving fans who believe in me and my team. Like God, I hope for their faith. What do you hope for?

Employee Engagement

Your fifth KPI is *employee engagement*. Business leaders have a vast number of options for measuring this. We use confidential team performance assessments. Whatever your tool for determining this metric, it must be done. I recommend two to three times per year.

After you have determined what winning is for your company, ask your team what winning is for them. Then ask, anonymously, how you are doing. Once you know, take immediate action. If you cannot change what they want, go to great lengths to explain why not and what you can do instead. If your team is not engaged, you are wasting them and the other resources available to you. Waste is not Godly.

Engagement for God is also measured in His top three KPIs. I noted them initially as:

1) Number of conversations about Jesus

2) Number of disciples led

3) Number of lives changed or raving fans

> **Regardless of conversion, making a friend and sharing your faith in Jesus and how He changed your life counts as a big win in God's blueprint**

The local church is helpful for this, but most contemporary newcomers to God's family will never set foot inside a church before knowing Jesus.

You must get outside the building. I prefer you do this at work. Make a friend; get to know them. When they are hurting, offer to pray. If they are receptive and show gratitude for your prayers, ask them if they have heard of Jesus. If they are open, tell your story. The rest is up to God!

Sharing your testimony might not immediately lead to someone's conversion. Sharing your faith in Jesus and how He changed your life counts as a significant win in God's blueprint. We saw this scripture earlier, but it bears repeating:

> And they have defeated him [the Accuser] by the blood of the Lamb and by their testimony. And they did not love their lives so much that they were afraid to die. (Rev. 12:11)

John, Jesus' best friend, teaches that your story and Jesus' shed blood overcomes all the brokenness of this world, forever. Your word, your story, is like a container for your faith that echoes into eternity. Telling your story is like drop shipping your faith to wherever the recipient goes afterward. Its a seed.

God brought me to His Son through more than just one person and one event. Although I will never forget Matt's story from January of 2010, going back over a decade prior, many others contributed along the way. Riding in my friend's car in the fall of 1997, I first heard a song called, *In The Light*, composed by DC Talk. It almost brought me to tears. Then my friend Travis gave me my first Bible, which I still possess, dated Feb 25, 1999. In 2002, not one, but two preachers in Boot Camp Sunday services taught me that Jesus was the only resurrected prophet in history. In 2008, I prayed to God alone, wanting Him to fix my mess of a life.

In 2009, and you won't believe this, three businessmen named, Brian, Brian, and another Brian were the first business guys to make it seem cool to be Christian. They brought me to multiple Sunday services. Finally, I surrendered to the Lord's call early the following year.

Every time you proclaim the Lordship of Jesus, you open the gates of hell a bit wider, leading the captives out. Matthew's Gospel reads:

> Simon Peter answered, "*You are the Messiah, the Son of the living God.*" Jesus replied, "You are blessed, Simon son of John, because my Father in heaven has revealed this to you. You did not learn this from any human being. Now I say to you that you are Peter (which means 'rock'), and *upon this rock I will build my church, and all the powers of hell will not conquer it.* (Matt. 16:16–18, emphasis added)

Your proclamation, just like Peter's, is your engagement into God's work.

Picking your top three to apprentice fulfills God's engagement metric and yours. Modeling Jesus, you must create a legacy for the company, department, or team to continue without you. Not only that, but you leave a legacy in God's Kingdom as well! When we get to heaven, we get to see how many lives were changed by our testimony, our tithe, our discipleship of others, and our faith!

Giving as a Percentage of EBITDA

Another *important metric to manage in your business is giving*. I prefer to measure this against EBITDA (Earnings Before Interest, Taxes, Depreciation, Amortization). As you grow your profit, your generosity should increase as well. God is 100 percent in control of outcomes, you control attitude and actions. Thus, as He increases your supply, your ability to bless others grows. Tithing against profit starts at ten percent. I've worked diligently over the years to increase our percentage.

Depending on our performance, we fluctuate between eleven percent and eighteen percent of profit to charity. Ten percent always goes to our home church. Sometimes more if there is a special project, but we enjoy giving.

Before I followed the Lord, I didn't really give, maybe sometimes to stroke my ego. Once saved, I initially gave simply out of obedience, but over the years, God has transformed my legal obedience into cheerful giving!

How much do you give?

In our personal household, we tithe and give on gross income, before taxes. We like to pay God before the government. Paying taxes (within reason) can be enjoyable if you realize the value your contribution brings to the country and the world. We are up to twelve percent consistently here. We have slowly worked our way up from 10%, to 10.1%, 10.5%, etc. I still have a goal of twenty!

Take it slow, but work to increase anytime you can. Generosity is contagious and brings personal health and joy to those that exercise it!

Personal Wellness

God's last KPI, is the foundation to your success in His work. It's *personal wellness*. You must stay T.R.I.M.

T.R.I.M. is an acronym for staying fit for duty in God's Special Forces. T stands for Time. You need to spend time with your best friend, who also happens to be your CEO, Jesus.

R is for Rest. You need to sleep every night; eat right, and exercise. All work taxes your body and brain. These activities—rest, food, exercise and family—will keep your body working correctly so you are not a burden to those around you.

I is for Immersion. Most of this book was teaching you how to fully integrate your faith, family, personality, and work into one unified effort to "go and make disciples." Total immersion is waking up, getting your coffee, and reading your devotional. You may prefer working out to praise music, or teaching, or preaching. Driving to work, play more praise music, teaching, and preaching. Or keep it quiet in the car. I do that frequently to see what God wants to tell me.

At work, your head is on a swivel to make a new friend. You don't need to make thousands of them, just one at a time. Depth is effective for relationships. Then at home, lead your family to prayer at night, and church on Sunday. If they have a class you can take, go to that once a week and volunteer a few times a month. That's only two or three hours at church, but you get great knowledge of God. Then pray or read His word before bed. If this sounds like too much, start small. One step at a time, but the more immersion, the more miracles you'll see happening around and through you!

Malcolm Gladwell, in his book, *Outliers,* described an angle on mastery. Get your 10,000 hours. For perspective, that would be approximately five years at forty hours per week. With total immersion, you are maximizing God's download with the time in your day, filling the space in your heart and head. If you don't know His word and story, you can't expect to know His handiwork. God has a plan perfectly laid out for you. When we miss the mark, He can fix it faster when we can actually recognize His activity.

How fast can you get your 10,000 hours?

For a trial run, consider this. Jesus rose from the dead after three days. Then he spent forty days hanging out with his friends. After ascending, there were ten days until the Holy Spirit came to the upper room. The Bible references forty quite a bit, so we will use that. It's a great time span to begin psychological change and develop new habits.

Here's your challenge. First, commit to a three-day food fast. No solid food, milkshakes, or purée. You can have coffee in the morning, chicken broth and most liquids, best to stick with water mostly, and no alcohol. At mealtimes, spend that time praying to God and keeping a journal of what you read, pray, and think. This is your reset button. Afterward, end your food fast, but spend the next forty days in total immersion, as I noted above.

You do not have to be perfect, but continue keeping alcohol to a minimum, eat and sleep right. Keep a journal, join our online community and check in with us.

https://jerryhowardinternationalcommunity.com/home

Pray for significant change in your life—whatever you need or want. Remember to determine the internal need you have, not the Ferrari. Look up what He says about that problem, pray, then watch God go to work!

Finally, M. Manifest is when you have developed a habit of spending time with God through His word and getting around other Christians further along in their journey than you. They need to be your guardrails for decisions. You cannot do this alone.

Once you know what God's word says, through intuition God will nudge ideas that build His kingdom. Be slow to act, and take big decisions and temptations to your guardrails. They will help you discern God's path. The circumstances in your life will start to manifest God's presence everywhere. Manifest is the most fun, but T.R.I.M. is a process that you need to stay with every day. Do not skip steps one through three and expect manifestation to occur, you will likely misinterpret what you see.

By doing this, by staying TRIM, God's armor revealed to us in Isaiah 59 will fit perfectly. Let's read:

> He put on righteousness as his body armor and
> placed the helmet of salvation on his head.
> He clothed himself with a robe of vengeance
> and wrapped himself in a cloak of divine passion. (Isa. 59:17)

In Ephesians, Paul writes:

> Therefore, put on every piece of God's armor so you will be able to resist the enemy in the time of evil. Then after the battle you will still

be standing firm. Stand your ground, putting on the belt of truth and the body armor of God's righteousness. For shoes, put on the peace that comes from the Good News so that you will be fully prepared. In addition to all of these, hold up the shield of faith to stop the fiery arrows of the devil. Put on salvation as your helmet, and take the sword of the Spirit, which is the word of God. (Eph. 6:13–17)

Without staying TRIM, your body and soul are exposed to the fiery arrows of the enemy. He will use any foothold to make contact. Assuredly, this will distract you, even depress or hurt you.

In the Marine Corps, we have very strict height and weight standards. I always made the BMI requirement, but because I lifted weights, I was heavier than the limit. At 5'11," I could only weigh up to 197 pounds. I typically weighed 205. After complaining to my dad, who was a Marine in the early '70s, he explained.

> **God's armor best fits the spiritually healthy version of you**

"In wartime, we do not have time to lift weights, drink protein shakes, or eat. We don't get to sleep much, and the stress of combat will strip you of everything but bones. If the Marine Corps standards don't keep you lean, when you go to war, very quickly your gear won't fit. That will cause a host of problems. Chafing at a minimum can make you an ineffective warfighter. They need you ready at all times. It's up to you to meet *their* standards."

God's armor best fits the healthy version of you. You can keep in spiritual and mental shape by starting with your body. Communing with God daily will take care of your soul and spirit. I'm definitely not physically where I was in the Marines, but I was spiritually bankrupt back then, and my soul was scorched. Today, I'm TRIM in the Lord and although not as lean, I can still do piggyback rides up the third floor at bedtime!

God's business KPIs and His favorite KPIs are designed to make you, your family, and your organization better prepared to fight against the prince of this fallen world. Not only that, but you get to participate in building the greatest Kingdom the universe has ever known. Your ROI is gained both in this world and the next. Straight from Jesus' lips:

> The seed that fell on good soil represents those who truly hear and understand God's word and *produce a harvest of thirty, sixty, or even a hundred times* as much as had been planted! (Matt. 13:23, emphasis added)

Did you notice the seed from this passage is all the same?

It's the soil that makes the difference! Focusing on God's KPIs fertilizes the soil of your heart. Sowing time, skills, and money into His kingdom produces the harvest you expect, but so much more—most of which you never dreamed possible! Read Mark's perspective:

> "Yes," Jesus replied, "and I assure you that everyone who has given up house or brothers or sisters or mother or father or children or property, for my sake and for the Good News, *will receive now in return a hundred times* as many houses, brothers, sisters, mothers, children, and property—along with persecution. And *in the world to come that person will have eternal life.* (Mark 10:29–30, emphasis added)

Now in this life, just like Job, and later in eternity, God will more than get you back for what you contribute.

Who's up for a 100-fold ROI?

Remember, He doesn't need you to accomplish His goals. He *wants* you to be a part of His project!

Where to begin?

No need to worry, overanalyze, or plan. Keep this book handy and start with one step. Start with your faith, even as small as a mustard seed. Take the first step. Pray, and let God show you the rest!

The Boardroom or Bible Study

For group discussion and individual journaling:

Jesus gets 100/100, and without faith it is impossible to please God. What would God's satisfaction rating be for you if he were human and didn't know your potential? What can you do immediately to get the score higher?

How intentional are you at making friends? What is your process? If you're not intentional, what can you change immediately?

What part of your walk with the Lord does someone desperately need to hear?

How much of an emphasis is giving financially to your family, team, or company?

Which part of God's armor, helmet, breastplate, belt, sword, shield, or sandals fits the worst? The best? What will you change to be TRIM?

CHAPTER 18

DISCIPLESHIP AT WORK: YOUR LIFE'S PURPOSE

> "Our chief want in life is somebody who will make us do what we can."
> –Ralph Waldo Emerson

Discipleship at work. I saved the best for last, friends! This is my favorite chapter, my favorite concept, and it's about two of my favorite people.

Other than Jesus, Joshua was my favorite OT Biblical leader.

I think Joshua and I (after my salvation) have similar tendencies. We're both military, love God's word, and are adventurous. But Simon (Peter) before Pentecost, reminds me so much of myself before Christ! What a knucklehead! He had a chip on his shoulder, wanted to fight everyone, spoke when he should've listened, the list goes on ...

When Jesus recruited Peter, many have thought, including myself for quite some time, that it was instantaneous. Most of us assume Jesus stepped into Simon's boat randomly and said, "Simon, throw your net over." The way it reads in Luke's Gospel is that Peter whined a bit but obliged and was blessed miraculously. The other three gospels indicate that it happened even faster.

Of course that did happen, but how was it that Jesus just stepped into his boat? As if He owned it?

Short answer, they already knew each other. Jesus' enlistment of Peter was far more intentional and strategic than we initially read. What's more, Jesus' approach to recruiting his number one guy lays a blueprint for world-class discipleship!

Whether on a battlefield or construction site, in an office or boardroom, everyone should be aware of your faith. Without ever implying that someone must follow my faith or is wrong if they don't, I simply reference mine anytime it is relevant to decision-making, but particularly in areas of morals and ethics.

If you are a Christian and you own a company or have a job, you may have heard of marketplace ministry. This term simply describes how individuals are recruited and apprenticed for Jesus while in a workplace setting. What I've learned is that everyone has heard of it, but it's not a focus in the overall institution of the church.

According to Dr. Steve Stells, pastor and founder of Hope Point Church, commented in his doctoral dissertation on the emotional health of pastors. He noted, most pastors when leaving seminary, feel unprepared. The primary area of concern for them is the business side of the church, running the operation. Thus, it's no surprise that marketplace topics are not commonly taught in the church. This shows that the church needs men and women like us to activate the community and lead the way! C'mon leaders, the church needs us!

According to Barna, media influences the church more than the church influences media. Barna also stated that a lack of sound biblical doctrine in seminaries makes pastors unprepared to lead. He also stated that the church structure was not Jesus' original design. Pastor Stells agrees that sound Biblical doctrine, Spirit led worship, combined with projects and activities to get everyone involved are the keys to growing the Body of Christ.

Strategically, that has been the layout of this book. I've given you sound doctrine in business and the Bible. I strongly encourage worship of God in all things. And we're wrapping up with how you engage others.

Remember, from the beginning, Jesus hung out with the business guys. It wasn't because they had money and He needed it. It was because He had limited time in His earthly ministry, and He probably got the biggest bang for his time in those places.

> **Jesus hung out with the business guys—not because he needed money—He was setting the stage for us**

Leaders, He was setting the stage for us! He knew the free-market system would eventually emerge and we would need a blueprint for how to operate outside a strict monarchy. Not only that, but everyone, at all levels of business can disciple others. Housekeeping staff to executive staff are all equally responsible for making a friend and telling their story about Jesus.

Hope Point Church in Chesterfield, VA, has a few buildings, multiple locations, and a fast-growing group of members, but its focus is discipleship. That's why it works. Paraphrasing, Stells teaches that we were created for four purposes:

1) Have a *relationship* with Jesus

2) To *worship* God

3) A *function* in the Body of Christ

4) To *multiply* ourselves, biologically and spiritually

He concludes by saying that doing anything else is either sin or on the road to it! With God's blueprint for world-class business, we accomplish all four of these purposes.

To disciple at work, as with all things human, Jesus is the outline. From his blog, Rick Renner gives a great commentary on the timeline of Jesus' recruitment of Simon, His rock. Furthermore, we can all execute this safely in the marketplace, without fear of scrutiny.

First, it is important to give Peter some grace. He was a business person and was very busy. Not only that, but there were many false prophets in Jesus' day. A few are referenced in Acts, but Jesus warns us:

> Beware of *false prophets who come disguised* as harmless sheep but are really vicious wolves. You can identify them by their fruit, that is, by the way they act. Can you pick grapes from thornbushes, or figs from thistles? A good tree produces good fruit, and a bad tree produces bad fruit. A good tree can't produce bad fruit, and a bad tree can't produce good fruit. So every tree that does not produce good fruit is chopped down and thrown into the fire. Yes, *just as you can identify a tree by its fruit, so you can identify people by their actions*. (Matt. 7:15–20, emphasis added)

This is a warning and filter. Before we outline the process, you'll want to know who you are dealing with. Discernment is key. False prophets use false doctrine, so make sure you fact-check people who claim to be following the Lord. Furthermore, look for fruit in their lives. Many examples were given in this book.

To summarize, there were four steps Jesus took, or four characteristics He exemplified, to get Peter's loyalty. iMPACT is achieved by at least two of the four, but preferably you will establish all four of these like Jesus. Here are the questions, through his actions, to which Jesus answered, yes.

Are you **HONEST?** That is, can I trust you?

John's Gospel reveals where Jesus started with Simon:

> The following day John was again standing with two of his disciples. As Jesus walked by, *John looked at him and declared, "Look! There is the Lamb of God!"* When John's two disciples heard this, they followed Jesus. Jesus looked around and saw them following. "What do you want?" he asked them. They replied, "Rabbi" (which means "Teacher"), "where are you staying?" "Come and see," he said. It was about four o'clock in the afternoon when *they went with him to the place where he was staying, and they remained with him the rest of the* day. *Andrew, Simon Peter's brother, was one of these men who heard what John said* and then followed Jesus. Andrew went to find his brother, Simon, and told him, "*We have found the Messiah*" (which means "Christ"). (John 1:35–41, emphasis added)

Repeatedly throughout the Gospels, we read where Jesus called Simon, son of John—meaning Simon was first a disciple of John the Baptist before following Jesus. Not only did John the Baptist, who Simon knew and respected, vouch for Jesus, but his little brother Andrew called Him the Messiah.

When your company does something great, or you personally impact someone positively, they have no trouble singing your praises. Thus, establishing trust can be done through others as well as your own actions. Jesus, being the master He is, raises the stakes at every interaction.

Jesus then established His next feature:

> Are you **PERSONABLE**? Can I connect with you?

Still in John's Gospel, right after getting introduced, Jesus does something most military people would like:

> Then Andrew brought Simon to meet Jesus. Looking intently at Simon, Jesus said, "Your name is Simon, son of John—but you will be called Cephas" (which means "Peter"). (John 1:42)

Simon certainly knew what Cephas meant. Right out of the gate, Jesus gave Simon his call sign! Call it a code name or secret identity if you want, but it's still cool. Maverick, eat your heart out. It's like joining a motorcycle club.

Men's Alliance, a fast-growing, fitness-based Bible study group, attracts men with the same approach. Big surprise, my call sign is "Impact." Although somewhat absent lately, due to my kids' sports schedule, I'm part of Spiritus Tribe in Chesterfield, VA.

Who doesn't want to be a superhero with a secret identity? Hundreds of millions of dollars in gross sales says we all do!

I'm convinced Jesus knew that Marvel and DC Comics would blow up the theaters today, so he kicked it off early, over 2000 years ago.

Once Jesus made friends with Simon, he had his attention, but not his complete allegiance. As a business person, Simon was likely curious about how effective Jesus could be as a Messiah. Jesus didn't fail to produce.

Like us, Simon was thinking:

> Are you **CAPABLE**? Can you do what you say?

Mark's Gospel answers:

> After Jesus left the synagogue with James and John, they went to Simon and Andrew's home. Now Simon's mother-in-law was sick in bed with a high fever. They told Jesus about her right away. So he went to her bedside, took her by the hand, and helped her sit up. Then the fever left her, and she prepared a meal for them. (Mark 1:29–31)

Afterward, Jesus continued to heal others, and it doesn't indicate he left Simon's house. Not only did Jesus take care of someone who could really add nothing to His cause, He did it up close and personal to Simon's life. Happy wife, happy life, as they say.

I wonder if Simon was thinking, "I'm so glad for my wife's mother to be healed, but I still gotta pay these bills, put food on the table. This is the priority."

What if Simon didn't believe and he just rationalized it to perfect timing? Sound familiar? How many times have you decided to grind it out at work rather than spend time with the Lord? Or your family? How many times have you dismissed a miracle as coincidence?

Since getting the bills paid is important, we've got to see the final step in establishing a true disciple. Here's what they want to know:

> Are you **RELIABLE**? Can I count on you to deliver for me personally?

This is where Jesus finally got Simon to recognize His supreme authority over everything that troubled him. Not long after Simon's mother-in-law was healed, Jesus showed up on the beach. This is such a great story. Luke writes:

> When he had finished speaking, he said to Simon, "Now go out where it is deeper, and let down your nets to catch some fish." "*Master*," Simon replied, "we worked hard all last night and didn't catch a thing. But *if you say so, I'll let the nets down again*." And this time their nets were so full of fish they began to tear! A shout for help brought their partners in the other boat, and soon both boats were filled with fish and on the verge of sinking. When Simon Peter realized what had happened, he fell to his knees before Jesus and said, "*Oh, Lord, please leave me—I'm such a sinful man*." For he was awestruck by the number of fish they had caught, as were the others with him. His partners, James and John, the sons of Zebedee, were also amazed. Jesus replied to Simon, "Don't be afraid! From now on you'll be fishing for people!" And as soon as they landed, *they left everything and followed Jesus*. (Luke 5:4–11, emphasis added)

Notice that Simon called Jesus "Master" before whining a bit. After everything he had seen already, it's no wonder. Now we know why Jesus could just step up into his boat like he owned it. Simon already knew He did—just like the cattle on a thousand hills!

After Jesus took care of all his needs, Simon called Him Lord and had no choice but to answer the call. Afterward, he spent the next three years learning how to live out his new name, Peter.

Honest, Personable, Capable, and Reliable are the characteristics need to make an iMPACT and recruit your top three, your Peter, James, and John.

Figure 7

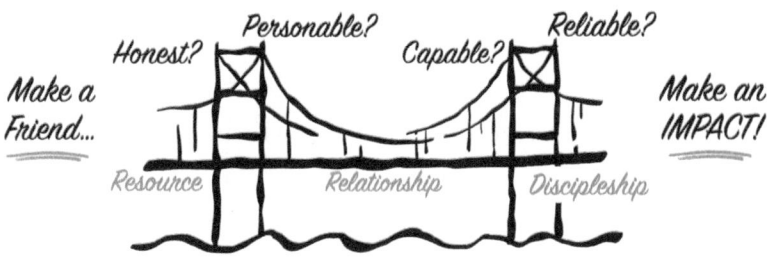

Note. Recruiting your Peter, James, and John requires building an *iNTREPiD iMPACT* Bridge.

Creating impact is like crossing a bridge. The pylons that hold the weight—being honest, personable, capable, and reliable—form the foundation and the structure of the bridge. The deck consists of the action words, relationship, resource, and discipleship.

Doesn't every Christian already have this responsibility?

We do. But those in leadership are held to a higher standard. Jesus is explicit in this duty:

> What sorrow awaits the world, because it tempts people to sin. Temptations are inevitable, but *what sorrow awaits the person who does the tempting.* (Matt. 18:7, emphasis added)

He does say there is grace for us who stumble. I'm so glad for that! Leadership is more important than mitigating your own sin, for which you can easily repent.

This is spiritual meat. Take extreme care that your stumbles do not lead others to sin; or worse, lead others to avoid Jesus. Your guardrails cannot be your disciples. Never vent or complain down the chain of command. Staying TRIM with the Lord, as I outlined in the previous chapter, is the best protection you can provide yourself as a leader.

Jesus recruits one of the best evangelists in human history. He had a process for making an impact.

We know the traits, but what actions do we see here?

While establishing yourself as someone with the aforementioned characteristics, I see three easy steps. First, he made a friend. He built a *relationship* with Simon, through his brother, and then with Simon directly. Jesus got to know him and his family. He knew them so well that Jesus got to pray for the mother-in-law to be healed. With a relationship, you can do this. Just be available and check in on your new friend. A simple text is fine.

"Hey [name], I'm about to pray for a few people, what prayer can I include for you?"

You ask that via text, and people really open up!

Relationships are so vital to putting you in a position of trust in their biggest time of need. Through you, Jesus could fill their boat! This action step is being a *resource*. When you help meet someone's needs, you speak to their heart. You fertilize the soil in which God's seed gets planted. You begin to carry the light, just like the Christian businessmen that discipled me so long ago. This is your true purpose at your job or business.

To summarize, you've built a *relationship* with someone for whom you truly care. You've been a *resource* for them to get through a challenge, both with prayer and material needs. Once God transforms their heart, you are ready to apprentice them. *Discipleship* is more than keeping the door open for questions, it's being proactive about including them in your life. Don't take it lightly, it is for the present, and for eternity!

You know I love the art and science of this. Just like our businesses and jobs, there are two parts. Qualitatively, the art of discipleship entails you exemplifying someone who is *honest*, *personable*, *capable*, and *reliable*. Quantitatively, your action steps are, make a friend with the intention of building a *relationship*. Please note, not everyone is ready for that. Respect their boundaries and be patient. Unless they are super excited about getting to know you, checking in weekly is probably plenty. You are going to do this with more than one person.

How do you know who God wants you to focus on? Here's how God reveals his intentions:

> Moses placed the staffs in the LORD's presence in the Tabernacle of the Covenant. When he went into the Tabernacle of the Covenant the next day, he found that *Aaron's staff*, representing the tribe of Levi, *had sprouted, budded, blossomed, and produced ripe almonds*! (Num. 17:7–8, emphasis added)

Just as Aaron's staff revealed God's choice for the tribe of Levi, follow the fruit of your efforts. In addition to your questions about them, take note of who asks lots of questions about God. That is fruit.

It is critical to remember you and your family's boundaries. Discipleship takes time. Don't overstretch yourself. One at a time is great. Stop at three. After you plant seeds for relationships, be ready and willing to pray for them.

God will reveal the right time to be a *resource* for their needs, and it may stop

> **Relationship, Resource and Discipleship**

at prayer. Be reasonable when you help. Do not second mortgage your house to get them out of bankruptcy. Remember the guardrails you established from the last chapter? Always check in with your mentors to ensure your blind spots are covered. Rarely does giving money to someone with money problems help them solve money problems. They need training and accountability.

Nothing in scripture indicates that Simon had trouble with his business, other than a bad night, so giving him lots of fish wasn't enabling. It provided the necessary push in his heart, one that ultimately led to him taking the first step to discipleship. If your personal and professional financial systems are right, you can teach your new friend. Teach someone how to significantly increase their personal balance sheet or take their financials from red to black. Watch how fast you gain massive influence!

After Jesus made a friend and formed a *relationship*, he became a *resource*. Only then did He spend three years running a *discipleship* program, teaching Simon to live up to his new name.

Look for a new friend every week. As the fruit manifests, hone in on your top three. Sometime in the next three years, encourage them to find three. After three years, get three more and so on.

Can you imagine how fast we could completely change the world if everyone had their three, six, nine, then twelve?

One generation, that's it!

The Boardroom or Bible Study

For group discussion and individual journaling:

How does it feel to know Jesus mostly hung around business leaders and working people? How does that change your perspective about the purpose of your work?

God created us for relationship, to worship, a function, and to multiply. Which area are you strongest in? Weakest? What can you change immediately to improve? What sin would that change lead you away from?

Who do you know that needs to be approached like Peter? What steps will you take to be perceived as honest, personable, capable, and reliable?

What can you do to establish a relationship? What need can you meet? How would you begin to train them?

CONCLUSION
NEXT STEPS FOR SUCCESS

Between gender confusion, abortion, and the rise of socialism, the enemy is producing his own fruit. It's time we started working hard again. Put down the game controller, leave the man cave and she shed. Yes, since there is no condemnation in Christ, this is Jerry calling you up to inspiration! We were not made to have it easy. We were created for battle. Heaven is "easy street." Those of us willing to fight right up to the end, when we are face-to-face with the Lord get a special place and a special reward in heaven. Paul writes in multiple places about the "judgment seat of Christ."

The BEMA seat, as it's known, is when you give an account for the work you did with what God gave you following salvation.

Did you get five talents?

That may have been lots of money, an inspirational skill set, or just lots of time on earth to make friends.

Maybe you received two talents? Or one?

It doesn't matter. What you want to hear is, "Well done my good and faithful servant."

Let's read what Paul says about the account we will give:

> For the Scriptures say, 'As surely as I live,' says the LORD, 'every knee will bend to me, and every tongue will declare allegiance, praise to God.' Yes, *each of us will give a personal account to God.* So let's stop condemning each other. Decide instead to live in such a way that you will not cause another believer to stumble and fall. (Rom. 14:11–13, emphasis added)

Here's another:

> So don't make judgments about anyone ahead of time—before the Lord returns. For he will bring our darkest secrets to light and will reveal our private motives. Then *God will give to each one whatever praise is due.* (1 Cor. 4:5, emphasis added)

I'm certainly one who struggled with all manner of debauchery both before and after salvation. Thankfully, God is still working in me to further my sanctification from sin. This is my favorite:

> So whether we are here in this body or away from this body, *our goal is to please him.* For we must *all stand before Christ to be judged.* We will each receive whatever we deserve for the good or evil we have done in this earthly body. (2 Cor. 5:9–10, emphasis added)

Circling back to the thief on the cross who called out for Jesus to remember him.

How many talents did he get? One? I would say he got 0.000001.

Did he use it effectively?

Let's look at Aaron's staff. What is the fruit?

We are still talking about it over 2000 years later! I'd say his reward in heaven is just as important as Paul's! Everything you do and say echoes into eternity. Make it count! Keep your heart right.

Recite this daily, change the pronouns (as I have), and memorize it:

> Today the LORD [my] God has commanded [me] to obey all these decrees and regulations. So [I will] be careful to obey them wholeheartedly. [I] have declared today that the LORD is [my] God. And [I] have promised to walk in his ways, and to obey his decrees, commands, and regulations, and to do everything he tells [me]. The LORD has declared today that [I am] his people, his own special treasure, just as he promised, and that [I] must obey all his commands. And if [I] do, he will set [me] high above all the other nations he has made. Then [I] will receive praise, honor, and renown. [I] will be a [leader] that is holy to the LORD [my] God, just as he promised. (Deut. 26:16–19)

Before you freak out about 'obeying all His decrees and regulations,' what did Jesus say?

Abide in Him and love each other. To be more specific, follow the blueprint and you win!

In our faith, in this spiritual war, winning is everything. Here's what winning really is and why it is so important to understand:

> Therefore, since we are surrounded by such a huge crowd of witnesses to the life of faith, let us strip off every weight that slows

us down, especially the sin that so easily trips us up. And let us run with endurance the race God has set before us. We do this by keeping our eyes on Jesus, the champion who initiates and perfects our faith. Because of the joy awaiting him, he endured the cross, disregarding its shame. Now he is seated in the place of honor beside God's throne. Think of all the hostility he endured from sinful people; then you won't become weary and give up. After all, you have not yet given your lives in your struggle against sin. And have you forgotten the encouraging words God spoke to you as his children? He said,

"My child, don't make light of the Lord's discipline,
and don't give up when he corrects you.
For the Lord disciplines those he loves,
and he punishes each one he accepts as his child."

As you endure this divine discipline, remember that God is treating you as his own children. Who ever heard of a child who is never disciplined by its father? If God doesn't discipline you as he does all of his children, it means that you are illegitimate and are not really his children at all ... God's discipline is always good for us, so that we might share in his holiness. No discipline is enjoyable while it is happening—it's painful! But afterward there will be a peaceful harvest of right living for those who are trained in this way. So take a new grip with your tired hands and strengthen your weak knees. Mark out a straight path for your feet so that those who are weak and lame will not fall but become strong. (Heb. 12:1–8, 10–13)

Follow Paul's instructions, use God's word, and the processes and steps provided in this book. Remember, we learned:

1) What it is, and Why we need Faith Driven Leadership and World Class Business

2) Applying the Big Ten for business

3) Managing your seven KPIs

4) Embracing God's favorite KPIs

5) Discipling others at work

Spend some time embracing God's priorities. Get yourself and your family moving in the right direction. The Big Ten for business should be applied to your home as well. Afterward, begin digging into your job or business.

Does your daily activity align with your Christian values?

If not, get to work applying the Big Ten and abide in the Lord, especially when you don't feel like it!

Simultaneously, get your team unified. Start managing your business and your life with God's favorite KPIs. Winning will manifest. Find some guardrails, mentors in your faith to keep you protected. Look for a few friends and apprentice them in the same principles.

We are business leaders, just like a dozen or so guys and gals who started this movement wandering around in the desert 2,000 years ago. Now we're billions strong, but every life that was changed, was changed personally, precisely, and purposefully. Everything we do is to change lives. That's it.

We are all counting on you. We need you to win. You are warrior kings and queens, priests and priestesses, in God's Special Forces, behind enemy lines! You are well-equipped but make sure your armor fits.

Most of all, remember, faith, leadership, and business are as inseparable as Father, Son, and Holy Spirit! On a daily basis, with every decision, you have an opportunity, an obligation, and a right, as a son and daughter of the Most High God, to execute faith-driven leadership according to God's blueprint for world-class business!

In closing, let's remember:

> Lord, my heart is not proud;
> my eyes are not haughty.
> I don't concern myself with matters too great
> or too awesome for me to grasp.
> Instead, I have calmed and quieted myself,
> like a weaned child who no longer cries for its mother's milk.
> Yes, like a weaned child is my soul within me.
> O Israel, put your hope in the Lord—
> now and always. (Ps. 131:1–3)

WORKS CONSULTED

An Inquiry into the Nature and Causes of the Wealth of Nations
> Smith, Adam. 1776. *An Inquiry into the Nature and Causes of the Wealth of Nations*. W. Strahan and T. Cadell: In the Strand.

American Leviathan
> Ryun, Ned. 2024. *American Leviathan*. Encounter Books.

Built to Sell
> Warrillow, John. 2012. *Built to Sell: Creating a Business that Can Thrive Without You*. Portfolio.

Coming Apart
> Murray, Charles. 2012. *Coming Apart: The State of White America, 1960–2010*. Crown Forum.

Getting China Wrong
> Friedberg, Aaron. 2022. *Getting China Wrong*. Polity.

Good to Great
> Collins, Jim. 2001. *Good to Great: Why Some Companies Make the Leap...and Others Don't*. HarperBusiness.

Honorable Design
> David, Jerry D. and Steve Stells. 2019. *Honorable Design: The Art and Order of Generational Transition*. Brookstone Publishing Group.

Outliers
> Gladwell, Malcolm. 2008. *Outliers: The Story of Success*. Little, Brown and Company.

Overruled: The Human Toll of Too Much Law
> Gorsuch, Neil and Janie Nitze. 2024. *Overruled: The Human Toll of Too Much Law*. Harper.

The Best Christmas Pageant Ever
> Robinson, Barbara. 1972. *The Best Christmas Pageant Ever*. HarperCollins.

The Rational Bible: Exodus
> Prager, D. 2018. *The Rational Bible: Exodus*. Regnery Faith.

Why the Jews: The Reason for Antisemitism
> Prager, Dennis and Joseph Telushkin. 2009. *Why the Jews: The Reason for Antisemitism*. Simon & Schuster.

World-Class Speed: The Proven KPI-Based Structure to Accelerate Business Growth
> Fuller, Peter C. 2024. *World-Class Speed: The Proven KPI-Based Structure to Accelerate Business Growth*. Expertise Publishing.

NOTES

Anti-Defamation League. (2023). "U.S. Antisemitic Incidents Soared 140 Percent in 2023 – Breaking All Previous Records." *Anti-Defamation League*. Updated April 16, 2024. Retrieved from https://www.adl.org/resources/press-release/us-antisemitic-incidents-soared-140-percent-2023-breaking-all-previous.

Bendavid, Eran, Christopher Oh, Jay Bhattacharya, and John P. A. Ioannidis. "Assessing mandatory stay-at-home and business closure effects on the spread of COVID-19." *European Journal of Clinical Investigation* 51(4). 2021. 1–9. https://doi.org/10.1111/eci.13484.

Cockram, Steve. YouTube. *Intrepid Impact Leadership*: Episode 9. July 28, 2023. Retrieved from https://www.youtube.com/watch?v=U8LzltJn3Ok.

Cretella, Michelle. A., Christopher H. Rosik, and A. A. Howsepian. "Sex and gender are distinct variables critical to health: Comment on Hyde, Bigler, Joel, Tate, and van Anders (2019)." American Psychologist. Oct 2019;74(7):842–844. Doi: 10.1037/amp0000524. PMID: 31580112.

Dhejne, Cecilia, Paul Lichtenstein, Marcus Boman, Anna L. V. Johansson, Niklas Långström, and Mikael Landén. "Long-Term Follow-Up of Transsexual Persons Undergoing Sex Reassignment Surgery: Cohort Study in Sweden." *PLOS ONE*, 6(2), e16885. 2011. https://doi.org/10.1371/journal.pone.0016885.

Hammer, Eric, William M. Knorpp, and Teresa R. Manning. "Should Virginians Pay for University 'Diversity, Equity, and Inclusion' and Leftist Ideology at Virginia Universities." Virginia Association of Scholars:2003. Retrieved from https://thejeffersoncouncil.com/app/uploads/2023/01/2023-DEI-report.pdf.

Heilbrun, Kirk, David DeMatteo, and Naomi E. S. Goldstein (Eds.). *APA Handbook of Psychology and Juvenile Justice*. American Psychological Association, 2016. 489–514.

Homeland Security Committee. "New: Investigation by House Homeland, Select Committee on the CCP Finds Potential Chinese Threats to U.S. Port Infrastructure Security." Homeland Security Republicans. September 12, 2024. Retrieved from https://homeland.house.gov/2024/09/12/new-investigation-by-house-homeland-select-committee-on-the-ccp-finds-potential-chinese-threats-to-u-s-port-infrastructure-security/.

Hughes, Siobhan. "Mark Zuckerberg Says White House Was 'Wrong' to Pressure Facebook on Covid." *The Wall Street Journal*." Last updated August 27, 2024. Retrieved from https://www.wsj.com/tech/mark-zuckerberg-neutral-politics-letter-election-2024-02b86372.

Institute of Medicine (US) Committee on Understanding the Biology of Sex and Gender Differences. "Exploring the Biological Contributions to Human Health: Does Sex Matter?" Wizemann, TM, Pardue ML, editors. Washington (DC): National Academies Press (US); 2001. PMID: 25057540.

Klett, Leah MarieAnn. "George Barna identifies biggest threats facing the Church: 'We've reached a time of Christian invisibility.'" *The Christian Post*. May 21, 2024. Retrieved from https://www.christianpost.com/news/george-barna-identifies-biggest-threats-facing-the-church.html.

Newcombe, Jerry. "The greatest story ever distorted: China trying to rewrite the Bible?" *Christian Post*. August 4, 2023. Retrieved from https://www.christianpost.com/voices/the-greatest-story-ever-distorted-china-trying-to-rewrite-bible.html.

Online Etymology Dictionary. (n.d.). Gender. Retrieved from https://www.etymonline.com/word/gender.

Parsons, John J. "Emet -Truth Hebrew Word of the Week." Hebrew for Christians. Accessed summer 2024. https://hebrew4christians.com/Glossary/Word_of_the_Week/Archived/Emet/emet.html.

Renner, Rick. "August 10: Coming to the Lord One Step at a Time." *Renner.org*. August 6, 2018. Retrieved from https://renner.org/article/coming-to-the-lord-one-step-at-a-time.

Renner, Rick. "What You Must Seek." *Renner Ministries.* December 25, 2019. Retrieved from https://renner.org/article/what-you-must-seek/ and https://www.youtube.com/watch?v=8vNLv5kmPJI.

Sylla, Richard, and Robert E. Wright. "Corporation Formation in the Antebellum United States in Comparative Context." Business History 55(4), 2013. 653–669. https://doi.org/10.1080/00076791.2012.741977.

Volz, Dustin. "Chinese Cargo Cranes at U.S. Ports Pose Espionage Risk, Probe Finds." *The Wall Street Journal.* September 12, 2024. Retrieved from https://www.wsj.com/politics/national-security/chinese-cargo-cranes-at-u-s-ports-pose-espionage-risk-probe-finds-1bc4b75b.

West, Rob. "The Business of Witnessing." Faith and Finance podcast. *Bott Radio Network.* November 9, 2022. Retrieved from https://bottradionetwork.com/ministry/faith-and-finance/2022-11-09-the-business-of-witnessing.

www.ingramcontent.com/pod-product-compliance
Lightning Source LLC
Chambersburg PA
CBHW022058120526
44580CB00017B/134/J